THE JEWISH MUSEUM NEW YORK

The Jewish Museum New York

Vivian B. Mann with Emily D. Bilski
Introduction by Joan Rosenbaum

SCALA BOOKS
In association with The Jewish Museum, New York

© Scala Publications Ltd
© Text Joan Rosenbaum, Vivian B. Mann, Emily D. Bilski

First published 1993 by
Scala Publications Ltd
28 Litchfield Street
London WC2H 9NJ

In association with
The Jewish Museum
1109 Fifth Avenue
New York
NY 10128

Distributed in the USA and Canada by
Rizzoli International Publications, Inc.
300 Park Avenue South
New York
NY 10010
All rights reserved

ISBN 1 85759 015 5

Designed by Alan Bartram
Edited by Tim Ayers
Produced by Scala Publications Ltd
Typeset by August Filmsetting, St Helens, England
Printed and bound in Italy by Graphicom, Vicenza

© Photos The Jewish Museum New York

Photo credits: John Back, Eric Baum, Geoffrey Clemens,
Coxe-Goldberg, Barry Friedman Gallery, Sidney Janis
Gallery, Lisa Kahane, Otto E. Nelson, William Nettles,
John Parnell, Eric Pollitzer, Joseph Sachs, Nicolas Sapieha,
Virginia F. Stern, Grant Taylor, Malcolm Varon, John
Weber Gallery, Graydon Wood, Alan Zindman

The Jewish Museum is under the auspices of
The Jewish Theological Seminary of America

Acknowledgments
Creating a book that involves the
holdings of several departments
within a museum requires the
cooperation of many people. I want
to acknowledge the unstinting and
devoted help of Sharon Wolfe and
Claudia Nahson of the Judaica
Department and of Susan Chevlowe
of the Fine Arts Department. The
contents of this volume benefited
from discussions with Joan
Rosenbaum, Ward Mintz, Norman
Kleeblatt, Susan Goodman and
Emily D. Bilski. Finally, Barbara
Treitel of the Visual Resources
Department was responsible for
many technical details.

Contents

Introduction 7
Joan Rosenbaum

Seeing the Future through the Light of the Past:
The Art of The Jewish Museum 9
Emily D. Bilski

Culture and Continuity: The Jewish Journey 22
Vivian B. Mann and Emily D. Bilski

Forging an Identity: Antiquity (1200BCE-600CE) 23

Interpreting a Tradition: The Middle Ages and After (800-1700) 28

Tradition: The Torah 31

Tradition: The Jewish Year 60

Tradition: The Sabbath 80

Tradition: The Life Cycle and Daily Life 86

Confronting Modernity: 1700-1948 100

Realizing a Future: The Contemporary World (1948-) 112

Index 128

1
Architect's rendering of renovated
building

Introduction
Joan Rosenbaum

The Jewish Museum is the shared legacy of over 4,000 years of history, and a contemporary mirror of an ancient and proud people. Founded in 1904, in The Library of The Jewish Theological Seminary of America, the Museum for nearly eighty-nine years has illuminated the Jewish experience, both secular and religious, demonstrating the strength of Jewish identity and culture. The collection and exhibitions offer a wide range of opportunities for exploring multiple facets of the Jewish experience, past and present, and for educating current and future generations.

The Seminary is a major scholarly resource for the Museum through its unparalleled library and excellent faculty. The Museum enjoys these and other advantages of its special relationship with the Seminary while operating with virtually total independence. It has a separate Board of Trustees and complete autonomy in its management and programs.

In 1993 the Museum completed a major expansion and renovation project, resulting in a doubling of the gallery space, new space for educational programs, and significant improvements in public amenities. Designed by renowned architect Kevin Roche, the expansion preserved the landmark 1908 Warburg Mansion which the Museum has occupied since 1947, and enlarged and reconfigured its 1963 List Building addition by extending the façade of the Warburg Mansion. The result is a greatly enlarged facility, with the unified appearance of an impressive late Gothic château (fig. 1). The Museum thus has become the largest Jewish museum in the world outside Israel.

The combination of art and history and the presentation of art and artifacts in the context of social history are what makes The Jewish Museum's exhibitions distinctive. Notable examples have included *The Dreyfus Affair: Art, Truth, and Justice, Golem! Danger, Deliverance and Art, The Circle of Montparnasse: Jewish Artists in Paris 1905-1945* and *Gardens and Ghettos: The Art of Jewish Life in Italy*. While these exhibitions have included art borrowed from institutions and private collections, the Museum's own collection forms the basis for exhibitions ranging in scope from the presentation of little-known archaeological artifacts from current excavations to avant-garde installations by young artists exploring issues related to their identity as Jews.

The Museum's diverse collection and rich exhibition schedule provide new opportunities each season to examine different aspects of the Jewish experience through program offerings for students, families and adults. Exhibition tours for school and adult groups, children's art workshops, shared family experiences, films, concerts, performances and lectures enable the Museum to serve audiences of unusual breadth and diversity.

As a key cultural resource for New York City and the world, The Jewish Museum continues to provide information, inspiration and stimulation to visitors, and a precious inheritance for future generations.

2

2
Cyrus Adler (1863-1940)

3
H. Ephraim Benguiat (d.1925)

3

Seeing the Future through the Light of the Past :
The Art of The Jewish Museum

Emily D. Bilski

Great nations write their autobiographies in three manuscripts: the book of their deeds, the book of their words, and the book of their art. Not one of these books can be understood unless we read the two others, but of the three the only trustworthy one is the last.
JOHN RUSKIN

In 1904, Judge Mayer Sulzberger included twenty-six objects as part of a gift of books and manuscripts to The Jewish Theological Seminary of America. These works of ceremonial and fine art were donated 'to serve as a suggestion for the establishment of a Jewish Museum.'[1] It is tempting to see in Judge Sulzberger's desire to establish such a museum, and in the great efforts on the part of the Seminary's professional and lay leadership to realize this wish successfully, a reflection of the insight articulated by Ruskin: a belief in the power of the physical object to communicate not only aesthetic values, but also the experiences, beliefs, aspirations and identity of a people. It is this extraordinary power of the art object that has fueled The Jewish Museum since its foundation eighty-nine years ago and continues to inform its collecting, exhibition and educational activities to this day. The Museum's original goals – the collection, preservation and research of material Jewish culture, coupled with presenting this material to the larger community in a compelling interpretative context in order to educate and stimulate – remain the priorities of The Jewish Museum today. And yet the unprecedented changes the world has witnessed during the last eighty-nine years have altered the significance and application of many of these goals. The history of the Museum can be seen as a reflection of the ever-shifting values and concerns of the world Jewish community, the American Jewish community and the art world, as the Museum has continued to evolve and adapt over the years.

The founders of The Jewish Museum recognized the opportunities that a museum would provide to enhance the Seminary as a center for research and teaching, as well as to facilitate the communication of Jewish culture and history to the general public. In their aims, the founders were part of the general *Zeitgeist*. Many of the major Judaica collections and Jewish museums in Europe had their beginnings around the turn of the century. There was a new consciousness in the air concerning the importance of artifacts used in Jewish ritual observances, as well as of objects that in some way related to Jewish history or personalities. The first great exhibition of Judaica took place at the Exposition Universelle in Paris in 1878 with the showing of the Isaac Strauss Collection.[2] It was followed by the Anglo-Jewish Historical Exhibition at the Royal Albert Hall in London in 1887. Jewish museums were established in Vienna (1897), Danzig (1904), Prague (1906) and Warsaw (1910). In Frankfurt, a museum was founded with the collection amassed by the Gesellschaft zur Erforschung jüdischer Kunstdenkmäler (Society for the Research of Jewish Art Monuments), an organization begun in 1900 by Heinrich Frauberger, the (non-Jewish) director of the art museum in Düsseldorf.

A number of factors contributed to this flowering of interest in the collection, preservation and research of Jewish material culture. Jewish emancipation, and the assimilation that followed, created an environment ripe for this development. In the first place, the departure from a strict adherence to traditional Judaism provided the psychological distance that enabled Jews to view ritual appurtenances as objects *per se*, apart from their religious functions. While retaining their ceremonial significance, the objects could also be seen as works of art, incorporating aesthetic as well as religious values. This objectivity was the essential prerequisite to moving a Torah shield or an eternal light from the synagogue into a museum.

Assimilation brought with it a decline in the use of many ceremonial objects for religious purposes. As synagogues fell into disuse, their rich holdings of artifacts were in danger of being damaged or altogether destroyed. People with foresight realized the necessity of taking quick action to save this aspect of their Jewish heritage, as was the case, for example, with Salomon Hugo Lieben who founded the Jewish Museum in Prague.

Yet another factor was the developing attitude within certain Jewish intellectual circles favoring a scientific approach to the study of Jewish history, philosophy and religion. The material manifestations of Jewish life could supply important data in the scientific investigations of Judaism, and the same stringent standards of inquiry could also be applied to a direct study of the objects themselves. It was hoped that collecting, exhibiting and

4

4
Museum objects on view at The
Jewish Theological Seminary,
1935-40

5
Hanukkah lamp
Eastern Europe, 19th century
Bronze, cast, 75.5 × 67.3 × 34.9 cm
The Rose and Benjamin Mintz
Collection, M 446

5

6

6
Curtain for the Torah ark
Istanbul (?), ca.1735
Silk, embroidered with silk and
metallic threads; metallic lace
border, 175 × 160 cm
The H. Ephraim and Mordecai
Benguiat Family Collection, s 4

studying Jewish artifacts in this way would serve a dual purpose: to educate Jews about their culture and help them nurture a respect for their traditions, while at the same time to enhance the non-Jews' appreciation and understanding of the Jewish heritage.

Such was the position of Cyrus Adler (fig. 2), one of the most passionate advocates in America of the scientific study of Judaism, who played a key role in the establishment of the Seminary, eventually serving as its president. Adler 'believed that Judaism, studied and taught according to the canons of modern scholarship, would enhance its respectability and that of its adherents... Not only would the non-Jew be prompted to give due accord to the heritage that nurtured Western religion, but the Jews themselves would understand the relevance of their 2,000-year-old tradition.'[3]

Adler, a founder of the Jewish Publication Society in 1888, the American Jewish Historical Society in 1892 and the Harvard Semitic Museum in 1903, was also active in the field of secular exhibitions and museums. In 1890, he worked on the preparations for the 1893 Chicago Exposition, and in 1893 he joined the Smithsonian Institution as librarian, rising to the position of assistant secretary in 1905. Adler's commitment to the study of Jewish culture and its dissemination to a wide public, coupled with his vast experience in the collection and exhibition of objects, uniquely qualified him to supervise the growth of the fledgling Jewish Museum. He provided the critical link between the Museum world and the Seminary, between a consciousness keenly attuned to the aesthetic and one devoted to the written word. Without Adler's crucial leadership, the Museum might never have been more than a small group of objects tucked away in a corner of the Seminary Library.

Fortunately, there were philanthropists who shared Adler's vision of a Jewish Museum and provided the financial support required to begin to build an important collection. Jacob H. Schiff, a director of the Seminary from 1902 until his death in 1920, had been a founder (with Adler) of the Harvard Semitic Museum. Schiff's son-in-law, Felix M. Warburg, another great supporter of the Seminary, was for many years a director of the American Museum of Natural History. Both men were art collectors, as well as patrons of Jewish scholarship. It was Warburg who supplied the first exhibition cases,

which were placed in the Reading Room of the old Seminary building on West 123rd Street. (Years later, it was Schiff's daughter and Warburg's widow, Frieda Schiff Warburg, who gave the Museum its own home when she donated her family's Fifth Avenue mansion in 1944.)

Building the Collections

Any discussion of The Jewish Museum and its contribution to American Jewish life must begin with its collection, the core of all its activities and its chief *raison d'être*. The first major acquisition by the Seminary was the Benguiat Collection, purchased in 1925. This distinguished private collection was primarily assembled during the nineteenth century by Hadji Ephraim Benguiat (fig. 3), an art dealer from Smyrna (Izmir), Turkey, who had undertaken a 'self-imposed family task to preserve... Jewish memorials of interest.' Benguiat's diverse collection, which included outstanding examples of Ashkenazi and Sephardi art, had been catalogued by Adler with I. M. Casanowicz in 1901. (fig. 6)[4] Adler described the acquisition of the Benguiat Collection in his remarks on the occasion of the Seminary's fiftieth anniversary:

In the building on 123rd Street, in a small way, there commenced to be brought together a few Jewish ceremonial objects. I think there were two or three cases. Before the present buildings were even projected, an opportunity came to secure a really notable collection. It was founded by the family of Benguiat, who spread over the larger cities in Europe and America. These men were collectors and dealers. They mostly sold what they collected with the exception of Jewish objects. In 1893, Ephraim Benguiat had a large shop in Boston, and I was looking for collections for the World's Fair in Chicago. When that exposition closed he transferred this loan to the Smithsonian Institution and later at his death, when it became necessary for his family to dispose of the collection, it was purchased by Felix M. Warburg with the assistance of a few friends, and placed in storage until such time as the Seminary could exhibit it. This is the origin of our present charming little Museum.[5]

As Adler made clear in his remarks, with the acquisition of the Benguiat Collection, the Museum needed a new physical space commensurate with its increasingly significant holdings. Thus in January 1931 the Museum of

Jewish Ceremonial Objects opened in the new Jacob H. Schiff Library Building on Broadway and 122nd Street as an annex to the Library (fig. 4).

The crisis in Europe in the two ensuing decades dramatically shifted the activities of collection and study of Jewish artifacts from the Continent to America, and invested these efforts with a new urgency and a terrible new significance. Three important components of The Jewish Museum's present collection are the direct result of the events of the Second World War and the destruction of European Jewry at the hands of the Nazis: the Mintz Collection, the Danzig Collection and the items presented to the Museum by the Jewish Cultural Reconstruction.

Benjamin Mintz began his collection as a professional art and antiques dealer in Warsaw, Poland. He was thus in a fortunate position to encounter and purchase some of the finest cultural artifacts of Polish Jewry. Judge Max N. Korshak, a friend, noted that 'it was quite easy for him to buy Jewish antiques and ceremonial objects but he did not have the heart to sell them and so over the years he gathered together a most amazing collection which, when he gave up his business, he stored in one of the large rooms of his apartment in Warsaw' (fig. 5).

Through the assistance of Korshak and others, Mintz and his wife Rose were able to bring the collection to New York for exhibition at the 1939 World's Fair. Although it was never exhibited, the Mintz collection was safely in New York when Hitler invaded Poland in September 1939, and was thus spared the fate of so many other pre-war Judaica collections. In 1947, Rose Mintz, then a widow, sold the entire collection to the Seminary for a relatively small sum in order to keep it intact.

Danzig had boasted one of Europe's earliest museums. Lesser Gieldzinski, a wealthy grain merchant, art collector and connoisseur, and friend to Kaiser Wilhelm II, donated his collection of Judaica to the Jewish community of Danzig on the occasion of his seventy-fifth birthday in 1904 (the same year as the founding of The Jewish Museum in New York), where it was housed in a special room in the Great Synagogue. By the autumn of 1938, conditions under the Nazis had deteriorated to such an extent that the officials of the Jewish community thought it best for all Jews to evacuate Danzig. The large sums of money needed to

finance this emigration were raised through the sale of Jewish communal property. The American Joint Distribution Committee arranged for the community's entire collection of Judaica to be 'sold' in America to raise some of these funds and, more importantly, to save it from imminent destruction. This collection consisted of Gieldzinski's donation, ceremonial objects from Danzig's five synagogues and others belonging to private individuals.

On 16 July 1939, these objects, filling ten huge crates, arrived at the Seminary. Among the conditions of the shipment was the stipulation that if a Jewish community were to be re-established in Danzig within fifteen years, the collection would be returned. If not, it would remain in New York 'for the education and inspiration of the rest of the world.' Today there is no Jewish community in Danzig – Gdansk, Poland since 1945 – but something of the vibrant community that thrived there has been preserved in the collection of ceremonial objects now housed in The Jewish Museum. The Jews in Danzig occupy a unique position in the history of the Holocaust – theirs was the only community with the foresight to save its treasures of ceremonial art and its archives (which were sent to Jerusalem).

At the conclusion of the Second World War, the disposition of Jewish cultural and religious property that had been looted by the Nazis and subsequently recovered by the United States Military Government was undertaken by the Jewish Cultural Reconstruction, Inc. (JCR). Founded in New York in 1947 as part of the larger Jewish Restitution Successor Organization, the JCR was headed by the prominent historian Salo Baron and managed by a distinguished committee. Whenever possible, materials were returned to the original owners, with the remaining items distributed to Jewish institutions worldwide. Along with looted books, Torah scrolls and archival materials were more than 5,000 ritual objects stolen from Jewish museums and synagogues (fig. 8). One hundred and twenty of these ceremonial objects, selected by the Museum's research associate, Dr Guido Schoenberger, entered The Jewish Museum collection in 1952.

The individual who left the greatest mark on The Jewish Museum's collection was Dr Harry G. Friedman (fig. 9). A prominent and philanthropic Jewish

7

Sampler
Holland or Germany, 1817
Maker: Zirle
Linen embroidered with silk threads,
35.5 × 20 cm
Gift of Dr Harry G. Friedman, F 690

8
Judaica recovered by the Jewish
Cultural Reconstruction; in storage
at The Jewish Museum

9
Dr Harry G. Friedman (1882-1965)

communal leader, Dr Friedman was a non-practising rabbi who had a brilliant financial career on Wall Street. His passion as a collector was to salvage the artistic creations of the Jewish past for the benefit of future generations. From 1941 until his death in 1965, Friedman acquired over 6,000 works of ceremonial and fine art, as well as archaeological material, which he donated to The Jewish Museum. Many items were purchased at the time of the Holocaust, as great European private collections were being disassembled and sold.

Dr Friedman's gifts to the Museum encompass objects from every place that Jews have lived and range from examples of folk art produced by anonymous Jewish artisans (fig. 7) to elaborate ceremonial works executed by some of Europe's finest silversmiths. Understanding that aesthetic judgments are often conditioned by one's culture, Friedman did not allow his selection of objects to be determined solely by contemporary taste or current value. He was concerned with the long-range and comprehensive preservation of Judaica.

This remains the Museum's primary collection goal. Many individuals have donated objects or provided funds to enable the Museum continuously to upgrade and expand its holdings. Some of these donors are well-known philanthropists who have been ongoing supporters, for example Felix and Frieda Warburg (fig. 10) and Albert and Vera List (fig. 11). Some have donated entire collections concentrating on one aspect of the Museum's holdings: the Museum's collection of 3,000 coins and medals, the most distinguished of its kind, is the result of the expertise and generosity of the late Samuel Friedenberg and his son Daniel (fig. 12). There are also many objects – discovered in a basement or a thrift shop, or even treasured family heirlooms – that are donated to The Jewish Museum by people who are neither extremely wealthy nor knowledgeable about Judaica, but who realize the vitality of the Museum and the importance of its collection for the preservation and dissemination of the Jewish artistic legacy.

Part of that vitality comes from an involvement with the actual making of art. As important collectors of contemporary art, Albert and Vera List for many years commissioned prominent American artists to execute an original graphic for The Jewish Museum on

8

9

the occasion of the Jewish New Year. Dr Abram Kanof and his wife, the late Dr Frances Pascher, enabled the Museum not only to guard the treasures of the past, but assured the continuous creation of Jewish ceremonial art. In 1956 they established the Tobe Pascher Workshop at The Jewish Museum, providing office, classroom and studio space for resident artists and their students. Founding director Ludwig Wolpert (fig. 13) was joined in 1961 by his colleague and former student, Moshe Zabari, who directed the workshop after Wolpert's death in 1981. Kanof recalls that the workshop 'was founded to apply the principles of contemporary design to Judaica . . . [It] continues to produce objects of quality and excellence according to the newest design philosophies but always in the service of the most ancient rituals and traditions.'[6] Through the generosity of the Lists, funds were made available for Zabari's works to enter the Museum collection.

A new dimension to the Museum's collecting and programming was added in March 1984, with the opening of the National Jewish Archive of Broadcasting. Created with a major grant from the Charles H. Revson Foundation, the Archive collects radio and television material that documents or dramatizes Jewish history, culture, current events and personalities (fig. 14). It provides a unique lens through which to view the Jewish experience as it is seen and interpreted through popular culture by both Jews and non-Jews.

The Museum's collections are a resource for other Jewish museums, Jewish communities, scholars and artists. Because of the impeccable provenance of so much of the collection, it provides a secure basis for evaluating the authenticity of other works of Judaica, especially today when forgery is rampant. The Museum has provided guidance for Jewish communities starting

museums, loans for Jewish and secular museums, and has circulated exhibitions internationally. Many of these have been seen in non-Jewish museums and have created an awareness in secular circles of the beauty and significance of Judaica. Artists have turned to the collection for information or inspiration for their work.

A Place to Show
The Museum's ability to present exhibitions and programs was greatly enhanced with the donation in 1944 of the Warburg mansion on Fifth Avenue and 92nd

10
Hanukkah lamp
Frankfurt-am-Main, 1706-32
Maker: Johann Adam Boller
(1679-1732)
Silver, cast, engraved, filigree, hammered and gilt; with enamel plaques, 42.5 × 36.3 cm
Gift of Mrs Frieda Warburg, s 563

11
Jacques Lipchitz (French-American, b. Lithuania, 1891-1973)
The Sacrifice, 1949-57
Bronze, 125.7 cm high, 61.6 × 61.6 cm base
Gift of Mr and Mrs Albert A. List Family, JM 16-65

10

16

Street, and the opening of the Museum in its new home in 1947. Moving the collections and installing them in the Warburg mansion was undertaken by the curator, Stephen Kayser. From 1945 until his departure in 1962, he shepherded the development of over eighty exhibitions, the acquisition of approximately 6,000 objects, ongoing research on the collection, and an impressive traveling exhibition program. Kayser's work set the standards for Jewish museums for many years to come.

In 1963, a three-story addition, made possible by the generosity of the Lists, was constructed to accommodate the Museum's growing programs (fig. 15). A major renovation and expansion, begun in 1990 and completed in 1993, has provided the Museum with an additional 30,000 square feet, effectively doubling the exhibition space, creating an education center and providing many more public amenities (fig. 1). For the first time in its history, the Museum is able to present a comprehensive interpretative exhibition on Jewish culture from antiquity to the present, drawn primarily from its own collections.

In assessing the Museum's impact on the American scene, one still looks with pride and wonder at the dazzling array of exhibitions of contemporary art held in the 1950s and 1960s. An exhibition in 1957, marking the tenth anniversary at the Fifth Avenue location – *Artists of the New York School: Second Generation* – presented the work of twenty-three young painters, including Helen Frankenthaler, Jasper Johns, Robert Rauschenberg and George Segal. In his introductory essay to the exhibition catalog, Leo Steinberg noted that though this constituted 'a departure from established practice,' there was a certain aptness to the exhibition of modern art at The Jewish Museum:

Both Jewry and modern art are masters of renunciation, having at one time renounced all props on which existence as a nation, or art, once seemed to depend. Jewry survived as an abstract nation, proving, as did modern art, how much was dispensable. I would also add that, like modern painting, Jewish religious practices are remarkably free of representational content, the ritual being largely self-fulfilling, rather than the bearer of a detachable meaning. Lastly, both Judaism and contemporary art established themselves by uncompromising exclusiveness. And if I said before that it is hard to be a modern painter, there is an old Jewish proverb to match that sentiment. Which possibly explains why many young Jews find it easy to become modern painters.

Artists of the New York School proved to be only the beginning of an exciting and ambitious exhibition program developed under subsequent directors Alan Solomon and Sam Hunter, showcasing the best avant-garde talent. There has been much criticism of the Museum during those years for concentrating on contemporary art that had no demonstrable Jewish content and 'abandoning' the Museum's original goals. In retrospect, these criticisms seem unfounded. Not only did the Museum continue to present exhibitions on Jewish themes, but it added to its permanent

11

collection of Judaica. The Museum's role in the discovery and promotion of artists who are now recognized as the greatest of their generation was a significant contribution to the development of postwar American art, and is but one example of a long and distinguished history of Jewish art patronage.[7]

Changes in both the art world and the Jewish world since the late 1960s have influenced the Museum's evolution and the way it has sought to implement its goals. With the proliferation of museums, alternative spaces and galleries devoted to the exhibition of contemporary art in New York and, indeed, across America, the Museum's role in this area lost much of its urgency. At the same time a new need was felt within the Jewish community, a need to explore the myriad components of Jewish identity. In the wake of the civil-rights movement, Americans from many different ethnic backgrounds began to question the desirability of the 'melting pot' ethic. Pride in the unique cultural legacies of parents and grandparents and the wish to keep those legacies alive for the benefit of future generations supplanted the earlier desire to blend inconspicuously into the general fabric of American life. For Jews, this trend was further enhanced by pride in the accomplishments of Israel and developments in Holocaust education. The necessity of coming to terms with the enormity of what had been lost lent new urgency to understanding and preserving what remained. For affiliated Jews, culture became another arena for the expression of the revitalization of their communities. For those Jews who had rejected religious traditions, Jewish culture and history became a medium through which Jewish identity could be reaffirmed. Clearly, The Jewish Museum had a new and important role to play as a resource for Jews from all points on the religious spectrum. The decision was made to focus once again on exhibitions that relate to the Jewish experience.

In our exhibitions, programs and publications, we continue to question the relationship between art and Jewish culture covering 4,000 years, embracing both Canaanite antiquities and the constructions of Frank Stella inspired by Polish wooden synagogues. Some exhibitions focus on particular Jewish communities, their history, art and communal life. For example, recent exhibitions have delved into these themes relating to the

Jews of Danzig, Frankfurt and Istanbul, Kaifeng, Italy, India, and the Jews of Ethiopia. We also present the work of individual artists, examine the state of Israeli or current American art dealing with Jewish themes, and document single historical events and their repercussions – for example, the Eichmann Trial. Often a whole new perspective can be gleaned by looking at a well-known subject through a different lens, as for example in the Museum's exhibitions examining the role of the visual arts in the Dreyfus Affair and exploring the visual interpretations of the golem legend. The Education Department uses these exhibitions to teach Jewish history and culture to 25,000 children annually, 60 per cent of whom come from public schools. Our location on Fifth Avenue – New York's 'Museum Mile' – attracts many tourists and visitors who would probably never seek out a Jewish museum or a Jewish institution of any kind. Both non-Jews and unaffiliated Jews can come here and experience something unique: the direct confrontation with objects embodying Jewish culture and history. The empathy and understanding acquired by looking at paintings made by a Jewish artist in hiding from the Nazis or by a child in the Terezín concentration camp goes beyond that gained by reading an historical account. Public programs enrich the exhibitions by providing new windows through which to examine the themes and ideas raised in the galleries.

A revived interest in all things Jewish coupled with the current visibility and popularity of museums in America has created a mood especially favorable for Jewish museums. This is reflected, to cite just one example, in the tremendous growth in membership at The Jewish Museum in recent years: from 4,879 in October 1982 to 11,400 in 1990. It is a propitious moment for an institution such as ours, an institution committed to fusing past and present with an eye to a healthy and vibrant future.

The foreword to the catalog of the 1957 exhibition of young New York artists declared: 'the present show intends to look forward instead of concerning itself with the past.' The Jewish Museum's winter 1986-87 exhibition, *Jewish Themes/Contemporary American Artists II*, offered an alternative aim. In his review of this exhibition, *The New York Times* art critic Michael Brenson called the show 'prophetic', observing: 'It is significant... for what it has to say about the possibilities

12

for art in the postmodern era ... It is again possible to make art ... that looks forward and backward at the same time. Only when both directions are present is there the possibility of a prophetic voice.'[8]

In those words we hear an echo of Cyrus Adler, who wrote in a letter dated 4 March 1894: 'The true prophet has ever been the one who saw the future through the light of the past.'[9] Brenson concluded his exhibition review: 'The relation of the past to the present and future is part of what this show – and The Jewish Museum – is all about.'[10] Exploring these relations and manifestations is a continuous process of discovery and growth to which The Jewish Museum has dedicated itself.

Note

I would like to express my deepest thanks to the following members of The Jewish Museum staff who graciously shared ideas, information and reminiscences, and who offered valuable counsel in the preparation of this article: Joan Rosenbaum, Director; Susan Goodman, Chief Curator; Susan Braunstein, Associate Curator; Moshe Zabari, former Director of the Tobe Pascher Workshop; Judith Siegel, Director of Education, and Andrew Ackerman, former Assistant Director. Thanks also to Grace Cohen Grossman, Curator, Hebrew Union College Skirball Museum, Los Angeles.

12
Medal of Elijah de Latas and his mother, Rica
Rome, 1552
Bronze, cast, 3.8 cm diameter
Gift of the Samuel Friedenberg
Collection, FBG 66

13
***Kiddush* cup**
Jerusalem, 1964
Maker: Ludwig Wolpert (1900-1981)
Silver, hammered and engraved,
19.1 cm high
Museum purchase, JM 67-74

13

14
Edward R. Murrow interviewing
David Ben Gurion on *See It Now*,
'Egypt-Israel', 13 March 1956, ©1984
CBS Inc.

14

Notes

1. Letter dated 20 January 1904, from Judge Mayer Sulzberger to
   Dr Cyrus Adler, then president of the Board of the Seminary.
2. The Strauss Collection was later acquired by Baron de Rothschild
   for the Musée de Cluny in Paris.
3. Naomi W. Cohen, 'Introduction', *Cyrus Adler: Selected Letters*, Ira
   Robinson ed.(Philadelphia and New York: The Jewish Publication
   Society and The Jewish Theological Seminary, 1985), pp.xxvii, xxix.
4. Cyrus Adler and I. M. Casanowicz, *Descriptive Catalogue of a
   Collection of Objects of Jewish Ceremonial Art Deposited in the U.S.
   National Museum by Hadji Ephraim Benguiat* (Washington D.C.:
   Government Printing Office, 1901).
5. Cyrus Adler, 'Semi-Centennial Address', *The Jewish Theological
   Seminary of America: Semi-Centennial Volume*, C. Adler ed., (New
   York, 1939), p.14.
6. Abram Kanof, 'The Tobe Pascher Workshop 1956-1986', *Moshe
   Zabari: A Twenty-Five Year Retrospective*, Nancy Berman ed. (New

York and Los Angeles: The Jewish Museum and Hebrew Union
   College Skirball Museum, 1986), p.6.
7. An examination of the role of Jewish patronage is long overdue.
   Among the future exhibitions being planned for the Museum is an
   investigation of the interaction between the Jewish dealers, gallery
   owners, critics, artists and patrons in fostering the avant-garde in
   Berlin during the first three decades of this century. A similar study
   could be undertaken on the New York art scene during the years
   after the Second World War.
8. Michael Brenson, 'Bringing Fresh Approaches to Age-Old Jewish
   Themes', *The New York Times*, 3 August 1986, 'Arts and Leisure'
   section, p.27.
9. Adler, *Selected Letters*, p.62.
10. Brenson, 'Jewish Themes', p.32.

15

Culture and Continuity: The Jewish Journey
Vivian B. Mann and Emily D. Bilski

The walls of a building often seem mysterious, hiding the activities that take place within. For an innocent visitor to the Jewish Museum, the extended façades of what was once a family mansion express gentility and grandeur, but may not immediately tell of the collections, facilities and programs that constitute the heart of the institution. The permanent exhibition, *Culture and Continuity*, focuses on a part of the Jewish Museum, its collections, which not only indicate the growth of the museum[1] but tell other stories as well.

One is the development of the Jews from a people like others, with their own land and religion, to a scattered people bound by religion and a common history. The collections also document art-historical and cultural interchange, the attempts by Jews to amalgamate their own needs and forms with the decorative traditions of host cultures. The existence, in the collection, of the same type of ceremonial object dated to various centuries attests to the continuity of Jewish belief and practice. In the modern period, paintings and sculpture by Jewish artists have become more commonplace than before. Their subjects encompass Jewish literary themes drawn from the Bible, reactions to modern Jewish history, and

secular themes held in common with other artists. Their art is Jewish in so far as it is art which mirrors the Jewish experience.[2]

To reflect the several ways in which Jewish art can be understood, the works in this book are, first of all, organized in historical periods: Forging an Identity: Antiquity (1200BCE-600CE); Interpreting a Tradition: The Middle Ages and After (800-1700); Confronting Modernity (1700-1948); and Realizing a Future: The Contemporary World (1948-). Where warranted, periods are further divided into subject areas. In all phases, the variety of styles used for objects having the same function within Jewish ceremony reflects the visual traditions of the various cultures in which Jews lived.

This organization reflects that of a new, permanent exhibition within the refurbished Jewish Museum. For the first time, the scope of the entire collection is mirrored in one exhibition. *Culture and Continuity: The Jewish Journey* seeks to explain how the definition of Jewish identity has changed in response to history. The works which testify to these changes are the subject of this book.

Notes

1. See Emily D. Bilski's essay, above, pp.9-21.
2. Vivian B. Mann and Gordon Tucker eds, *The Seminar on Jewish Art. January-September 1984. Proceedings* (New York, 1985.), p.10.

Forging an Identity:
Antiquity (1200BCE - 600CE)
This section was co-authored by Susan Braunstein

Jewish identity has been defined since antiquity by an intense bond to the land of Israel and by the worship of one God. Yet in the ancient world the people of Israel underwent radical changes – of location, government and forms of worshipping God. At the beginning of the period, Israelites ruled their own land and worshipped by means of animal sacrifice; kings and priests led them. Ultimately, they became Jews, living under foreign rule in communities scattered throughout the ancient world, worshipping through prayer and Bible study, guided by rabbis.

Conquest by foreign armies and interaction with neighboring cultures forced the Israelite community to ask: How can we survive without independence? How can we worship? What should be assimilated from other cultures, and what rejected? The answers formulated in the ancient period continue to provide the basis for Judaism's survival in adverse conditions and diverse places.

In archaeological terms, the period from 1200 to 586BCE (the date of the destruction of the First Temple in Jerusalem) is the Iron Age, deriving its name from the first widespread use of iron for tools, weapons and jewelry. Early in this period, pottery was derived from Canaanite prototypes, but later Israelites developed distinctive forms and decoration (fig. 16). The period ended with the Babylonian Conquest and the exile of the leading inhabitants of ancient Israel. In 539BCE, Cyrus,

King of Persia, allowed some of these Jews to return to Jerusalem. Those who did rebuilt the Temple between 519 and 515BCE, inaugurating the Second Temple Period, during which a strong Hellenistic influence on art and thought emerged. One result was the widespread consumption of luxury goods such as glass and jewelry (figs 17 and 20). The destruction of the Temple by the Romans in 70CE, the event which closes the Second Temple Period, was marked by the minting of Judaea Capta coins (fig. 19, 19a).

Many Israelites were taken to Rome as slaves; most were eventually freed and joined the Roman Jewish community. Jewish burials, like those of Christians and pagans of the period, largely took place in catacombs. Graves were often marked by tombstones which, stylistically and iconographically, resembled those of the Early Christians (fig. 23). These works of the Republican period attest to the Jewish adoption of Roman forms and symbols.

Catacomb inscriptions indicate the existence of twelve synagogues in ancient Rome. After the Second Temple was destroyed, the synagogue, which had evolved earlier as an institution for the reading and study of the Torah, became the primary Jewish religious institution. The end of Temple worship, and its complete replacement by Torah reading and interpretation, marks the final transformation from Israelite religion to rabbinic Judaism.

16

**Jewelry of the Second Temple
Period**

Top left:

(a) **Pair of earrings**
Eastern Mediterranean, Hellenistic
to Early Roman Periods, 4th century
BCE-1st century CE
Gold, hammered, granulated and
drawn wire, 2.85 cm long, 1.3 cm wide
Gift of the Betty and Max Ratner
Collection, 1981-211, 212

Bottom left:

(b) **Ear or nose ring**
Eastern Mediterranean, probably
Hellenistic Period, 4th-1st century
BCE
Gold, cast, granulated, cut sheet-
metal and twisted wire, 1.4 cm
diameter, head: 0.4 cm diameter
Gift of the Betty and Max Ratner
Collection, 1981-131

Center:

(c) **Pendant**
Eastern Mediterranean, probably
Roman Period, 1st century BCE-4th
century CE
Gold, hammered, braided,
granulated; opal (?) and pearl, drilled,
8.5 cm long
Gift of the Betty and Max Ratner
Collection, 1981-99

Top right:

(d) **Earring**
Eastern Mediterranean
Hellenistic-Roman Periods, 2nd
century BCE-4th century CE
Gold, wire and bead; stone
(emerald?), polished and drilled,
2.9 cm long
Gift of the Betty and Max Ratner
Collection, 1981-100

Bottom right:
(e) **Earring**
Eastern Mediterranean,
probably Roman Period,
50BCE-300CE
Gold, hammered and drawn wire,
1.6 cm wide, 1.4 cm long
Gift of the Betty and Max Ratner
Collection, 1981-210

16
Iron Age pots

Front row, left to right:

(a) **Spouted juglet**
Israel, Iron II A-C, 1000-586BCE
Clay, wheel-turned, pulled handle,
applied spout, burnished, fired and
painted, 13.7 cm, 9 cm diameter
Gift of Joy Ungerleider, JM 249-68

(b) **Decanter**
Lachish excavation, tomb 106
Iron II C, 800-586BCE
Clay, wheel-turned, pulled handle,
slipped, wheel-burnished and
fired, 17.6 cm, 11.1 cm diameter
Archaeology Acquisition Fund,
JM 12-73.263

(c) **Spouted strainer jug**
Israel, Iron II A-C, 1000-700BCE
Clay, wheel-turned, handle and spout
hand-made, pierced, slipped, hand-
burnished and fired, 23.4 cm, 15.1 cm
diameter, spout length 8 cm
Gift of Joy Ungerleider, JM 233-68

Back row, left to right:

(d) **Decanter**
Israel, Iron II C, 800-586BCE
Clay, wheel-turned, pulled handle,
slipped, wheel-burnished and fired,
27.3 cm, 18.9 cm diameter
Archaeology Acquisition Fund,
JM 12-73.145

(e) **Amphoriskos**
Lachish excavation, tomb 1002
Iron II C, 800-700BCE
Clay, wheel-turned, pulled handles,
slipped, fired and painted, 20.1 cm,
9.9 cm diameter
Archaeology Acquisition Fund,
JM 12-73.443

(f) **Pilgrim flask**
Israel, Iron II C, 800-586BCE
Clay, wheel-turned, pulled handles,
wheel-burnished and fired,
31.7 × 22.5 cm
Gift of the Betty and Max Ratner
Collection, 1981-162

17

18

18
Tripod mortar and pestle
Israel, Early Roman Period,
50BCE-70CE
Basalt, ground and incised, 11 × 25 cm
Gift of the Betty and Max Ratner
Collection, 1982-24

19

19A

19, 19A
***Judaea Capta* coin: Emperor**
Vespasian
Rome, 71 CE
Gold, 7.1 gm
The Jewish Museum, x 1983-88

20
Glass bottles of the Second Temple Period

Front row, left to right:

(a) **Bottle**
Eastern Mediterranean, Early-Middle Roman Period, late 1st-3rd century CE
Glass, free-blown and wheel-incised, 14.5 cm high, 10.2 cm diameter
Gift of the Betty and Max Ratner Collection, 1981-72

(b) **Piriform bottle**
Eastern Mediterranean, Early Roman Period, early 1st century BCE
Glass, free-blown and banded,

10.1 cm high, 4.6 cm diameter
Gift of Elaine and Harvey Rothenberg, JM 94-79

(c) **Jar**
Eastern Mediterranean, Early Roman Period, 1st century CE
Glass, mold-blown and thread handles, 9 cm high, 4.4 cm diameter
Gift of Elaine and Harvey Rothenberg, JM 93-79

(d) **Piriform bottle**
Eastern Mediterranean, Early Roman Period, 1st century CE
Glass, free-blown, 10.5 cm high, 6.8 cm diameter
Gift of the Betty and Max Ratner Collection, 1981-83

(e) **Globular bottle**
Eastern Mediterranean, Early Roman Period, 1st century CE
Glass, free-blown, 10.9 cm high, 6.6 cm diameter
Gift of Judith Riklis, 1981-273

Back row, left to right:

(f) **Globular bottle**
Eastern Mediterranean, Early Roman Period, 1st century CE
Glass, free-blown and wheel-incised, 12.1 cm high, 6.8 cm diameter
Gift of Judith Riklis, 1981-269

21

22

23

(g) **Large globular bottle**
Eastern Mediterranean, Middle
Roman Period, 2nd-3rd century CE
Glass, free-blown, 25 cm high,
19.6 cm diameter
Gift of the Betty and Max Ratner
Collection, 1981-79

(h) **Cylindrical jug**
Eastern Mediterranean,
Middle Roman Period,
late 1st-2nd century CE
Glass, free-blown, wheel-incised and
thread handle, 19.5 cm high, 8 cm
diameter
Gift of the Betty and Max Ratner
Collection, 1981-70

21
Bar Kokhba coin
Ancient Israel, 133-34CE
Silver, 2.8 cm diameter
Gift of Mr and Mrs Robert Wagner,
JM 28-75

22
Eight-wick oil lamp
Ancient Israel, 3rd-5th century CE
Terracotta, mold-formed,
5.1 × 9.2 × 13.6 cm
Gift of the Betty and Max Ratner
Collection, 1981-75

23
Burial plaques

(a) Venosa (?), 4th-5th century
Marble, incised, 24.1 × 28.2 × 2.9 cm
Gift of Mr Samuel Friedenberg,
JM 3-50

(b) Rome, 2nd-3rd century
Marble, carved and painted,
29.5 × 26.5 × 3 cm
Gift of Henry L. Moses in memory
of Mr and Mrs Henry
P. Goldschmidt, JM 5-50

(c) Rome, 2nd-3rd century
Marble, incised, 24.2 × 25.3 × 2.2 cm
Gift of Dr Harry G. Friedman, F 4717

Interpreting a Tradition:
The Middle Ages and After (800-1700)

From the end of antiquity until the dawn of the modern age, Jews established communities all over the world. Jewish culture flourished because of its flexibility and resilience, despite legal restrictions and persecutions. Local political, economic, climatic and cultural conditions influenced the development of individual communities, resulting in an extraordinarily diverse Jewish culture throughout Europe and the Near East.

Apart from external factors, Judaism promoted an ongoing internal dialogue about the meaning of the Jewish tradition. The establishment of permanent Jewish communities along the Rhine and on the Iberian peninsula during the ninth century eventually gave rise, by the end of the Middle Ages, to two major religious traditions: the Ashkenazi and the Sephardi (terms based on the Hebrew names for Germany and Spain). With the expulsion of Jews from many German cities in the sixteenth century and their eastward migration, the Ashkenazic tradition became established in eastern Europe. A third major tradition of Jewish practice arose in the lands east of Ancient Israel, whose Jewish inhabitants migrated directly from their ancient homeland without a European sojourn. They are known as the *edot ha-mizrah*, the eastern communities.

Most of the Jews of the Ottoman Empire, for example, were Sephardim, descendants of those expelled from Spain and Portugal in 1492 and 1497. Sultan Bayezid II welcomed the refugees, whose excellent education and knowledge of industry, technology and medicine were important contributions to the developing Empire.

The art of Ottoman Jewry includes works traditional among the Jews of the Iberian peninsula, such as the illuminated marriage contract (fig. 24) and the knotted pile rug used to decorate the Torah ark (fig. 36), as well as types developed in response to Ottoman culture. The Ottoman emphasis on de luxe embroidery with silver, gold and silk threads as an art form influenced Jewish women to create elaborate textiles for ceremonial use (figs. 25 and 26). Occasionally, comparable ceremonies among Muslims and Jews led to Jewish adaptation of an Islamic type, for example the *tombak* ewer and basin once owned by a Muslim that was later used by the Benguiat family of Smyrna for ritual handwashing at the home service for Passover (fig. 27).

The works of Jewish ceremonial art illustrated in this section, while reflecting the customs of diverse Jewish communities and the artistic influences of their surrounding cultures, also express shared values. Each was created to enable Jews to fulfill the requirements of Jewish Law. They also embody the principle of *hiddur mitzvah*—enhancing the performance of a commandment by using an object of beauty. This concept originated in a rabbinic interpretation of a biblical verse, part of the song that Moses sang in gratitude after the Israelites crossed the Red Sea: 'This is my God and I will glorify Him' (Ex. 15:2).

24
Marriage contract of Yosef, son of Moshe Tarica, and Rivka, daughter of Moshe Soriano (?)
Rhodes, 1830
Ink and gouache on parchment,
85.7 × 64.1 cm
The Jewish Museum, s 142

25

25

Amuletic headdress for the mother of a newborn

Ottoman Empire, ca.1850
Silk, embroidered with metallic
threads, tinsel and sequins; metallic
lace, 16.5 × 28.5 cm
Gift of Dr Harry G. Friedman, F 646

26

Cushion cover

Istanbul, late 17th or early 18th
century
Silk, embroidered with metallic
threads, metallic braid, 48.2 × 55.2 cm
Gift of Dr Harry G. Friedman, F 5465

27

Ewer and basin used at Passover

Istanbul, 1840-50
Copper, gilt (*tombak*), repoussé,
punched and engraved
Ewer: 32.4 × 21.6 cm
Basin: 12.3 × 36.8 cm
The H. Ephraim and Mordecai
Benguiat Family Collection, s 77 a-c

26

27

Tradition: The Torah

All aspects of traditional Jewish life are based on the Torah, the first five books of the Hebrew Bible, and on rabbinic interpretations of its text. Jewish customs and ritual express both an ongoing emphasis on interpretation of the Torah (which continues into our own day), and the impact of the diverse times and places in which Jews have lived.

Over the centuries, Jews created a ritual context for protecting and decorating the Torah scroll. It is generally housed in a cabinet that is set in or against one wall of a synagogue, traditionally the wall oriented toward Jerusalem (figs. 29-32). The Torah scroll is removed from the Torah ark or niche and carried to the reader's desk (figs. 63-64) for public reading on Sabbaths, Mondays and Thursdays, and on festivals when these occur on the remaining days of the week (fig. 28).

Jewish reverence for the Torah inspired the creation of objects to safeguard its sanctity and to protect it from damage: mantles (figs. 39, 40, 55-57); binders (figs. 58, 60-62); cases, *tikim* (figs. 50 and 54), and the pointer (figs. 39 and 59). Other objects facilitate the public reading of the Torah (shields, figs. 49, 51-53), or emphasize its majesty (crowns and finials, figs. 41-48).

Varying forms for Torah ornaments developed among Eastern, Sephardi and Ashkenazi Jews that were maintained long after the dispersion of the original communities. Carried to new areas of settlement, these distinctive forms embody the Talmudic saying: 'Give heed to the customs of your ancestors.'

28

28
Solomon Alexander Hart
(British, 1806-81)
*The Feast of the Rejoicing of the Law at
the Synagogue in Leghorn, Italy*, 1850
Oil on canvas, 141.3 × 174.6 cm
Gift of Mr and Mrs Oscar Gruss,
JM 28-55

29
Torah ark
Urbino, ca.1500, refurbished 1624
Wood, carved, painted, gilt and
stained, 239 × 279 × 86.4 cm
The H. Ephraim and Mordecai
Benguiat Family Collection, s 1431

30
Portion of a synagogue wall
Isfahan (?), Persia, 16th century
Faience tile mosaic, 264.2 × 472.4 cm
Gift of Adele and Harry
G. Friedman, Lucy and Henry
Moses, Miriam Schaar Schloessinger,
Florence Sutro Anspacher, Lucille
and Samuel Lemberg, John
S. Lawrence, Louis A. Oresman, and
Khalil Rabenou, F 5000

29

30

31
Torah ark
Westheim bei Hassfurt, Bavaria, 18th
century
Pinewood, carved and painted;
fabric, embroidered with metallic
threads, 287 × 160 cm
Gift of Arthur Heiman, JM 138-47

32
**Torah ark from Adath Jeshurun
Synagogue**
Sioux City, Iowa, 1899
Maker: Abraham Schulkin
Carved pine, stained and with gold-
colored bronze paint,
305 × 244 × 76 cm
Gift of the Jewish Federation of
Sioux City, Iowa, JM 48-56

31

33
Curtain for the Torah ark
Venice, 1680/81
Maker: Simḥah, wife of Menaḥem
Levi Meshullami
Silk, embroidered with silk and
metallic threads, metallic fringe,
216.1 × 140.1 cm
Gift of Professor Neppi Modona,
Florence, through Dr Harry
G. Friedman, F 2944

34

33

35

36

36

34
Curtain for the Torah ark
Italy, 1643/44
Silk and silk damask, appliquéd and
embroidered with metallic threads,
163 × 112 cm
Gift of Dr Harry G. Friedman, F 3580

35
Curtain for the Torah ark
Venice (?), Italy, 1698/99
Maker: Leah Ottolenghi
Linen, embroidered with silk and
metallic threads, 184 × 122 cm
Gift of Dr Harry G. Friedman, F 3432

36
Curtain for the Torah ark
Gördes, early 19th century
Wool and cotton, in Gördes knot,
161 × 119 cm
Gift of Dr Harry G. Friedman, F 5182

37
Curtain and valance for the Torah ark
Galicia, 1831/32
Weave-patterned silk and velvet, embroidered with silk and metallic threads; appliquéd with metallic bobbin lace, silver non-woven openwork (Yiddish: *shpanyer*); stamped metal forms; foils
Curtain: 105 × 74 cm
Valance: 34 × 80 cm
Gift of Samuel Friedenberg, JM 53-49 a,b

37

38
Curtain and valance for the Torah ark
Bavaria, 1772/73
Maker: Jacob Koppel Gans
Velvet, cut and uncut, embroidered with metallic and silk threads
Curtain: 213.4 × 163.8 cm
Valance: 95.3 × 171.5 cm
Gift of Dr Harry G. Friedman, F 1285 a,b

39   40

39
Dressed Ashkenazi Torah scroll

(a) **Torah mantle**
Prussia, 1713-50
Satin, embroidered with silks and
metallic thread; lower edge, metallic
braid and velvet, 66 × 38 cm
Gift of the Danzig Jewish
Community, D 254

(b) **Pair of finials**
Berlin, 1788-1802
Maker: AG, probably August
Ferdinand Gentzmer

Silver, cast, cut-out, chased, engraved,
hammered, parcel-gilt, 70 × 40.7 cm
Gift of the Danzig Jewish
Community, D 184 a,b

(c) **Torah pointer**
Danzig, 1766-1812
Maker: possibly Johann Christian
Franck
Silver, cast and engraved, 28 cm long,
3 cm diameter
Gift of the Danzig Jewish
Community, D 31

40
Dressed Sephardi Torah scroll from the Ottoman Empire

(a) **Torah mantle**
Istanbul, ca.1881
Velvet, embroidered with metallic and silk threads, 93 × 50 × 27 cm
The H. Ephraim and Mordecai Benguiat Family Collection, s 19

(b) **Torah shield**
Ottoman Empire, 1863-64
Silver, cast, repoussé, engraved, parcel-gilt and nielloed, 29 × 25.4 cm
Division of Community Life, National Museum of American History, Smithsonian Institution, Washington DC, 154.990

(c) **Torah finial** (left)
Ottoman Empire, late 19th century
Silver, raised, repoussé, ajouré and engraved, 38.9 × 11.1 cm
Gift of Dr Harry G. Friedman, F 3174

(d) **Torah finial** (right)
Ottoman Empire, late 19th century
Silver, raised, engraved, ajouré and stamped, 39 × 11.5 cm
Gift of Dr Harry G. Friedman, F 1956

41
Torah finials
Mantua, 17th-18th century
Silver, cast, repoussé and engraved, 61 × 12.5 cm
Gift of Samuel and Lucille Lemberg, JM 20-64 a,b

42
Torah finials
Frankfurt-am-Main, ca.1720
Maker: Jeremias Zobel (1670-1741)
Silver, cast, repoussé, stippled, engraved and gilt, 45.7 × 17.8 cm
Gift of Dr Harry G. Friedman, F 3685 a,b

43
Torah finials
British Colonies, probably North America or the West Indies, ca.1800
Maker: Master ER or FR
Silver, cast, cut-out, parcel-gilt, engraved and punched, 45.1 × 14.3 cm
Gift of Jacobo Furman in memory of his wife Asea, 1992-144 a,b

41

43

42

44

45

44
Torah finials
France, 1876 (inscription date)
Silver, cast, cut-out, engraved,
repoussé, stamped and parcel-gilt,
24.1 × 7 cm
The Morris and Eva Feld Judaica
Acquisitions Fund, 1981-27 a,b

45
Torah finials
Persia, 1851/52 (inscription date)
Silver, repoussé, engraved and
chased, 28.5 cm high
Gift of Dr Harry G. Friedman,
F 3726 a,b

46
Torah crown
Lemberg (Lvov), Poland, 1764/65
and 1773 (inscription dates)
Silver, cast, repoussé, cut-out,
engraved, parcel-gilt, semi-precious
stones, glass stones, 49 × 22 cm
Gift of Dr Harry G. Friedman, F 2585

47

48

44

47
Torah crown
Algeria or Tunisia, 1898/99
Silver, pressed and chased, 82 cm
(open)
Judaica Acquisitions Fund, 1990-13

48
Torah crown
Berlin, 1779
Maker: Joachim Hübener
(ca.1705-1780)
Silver, cast, repoussé, engraved and
parcel-gilt, semi-precious stones,
glass stones, 40.6 × 22.2 cm
Gift of the Danzig Jewish
Community, D 61

49
Torah shield
Augsburg, ca.1715
Maker: Zacharias Wagner
(ca.1680-1733)
Silver, cast, repoussé, engraved and
gilt, 42.2 × 30.3 cm
Gift of Dr Harry G. Friedman, F 70c

49

50
Torah case (*tik*)
(a) North Africa, 19th century
Wood, carved and inlaid with shell,
76.2 cm high
Purchased from the Jewish
Community of Malta, 1984-70 a

(b) **Pair of Torah finials**
Italy, 19th century
Silver, cast, openwork and engraved,
48.1 cm high, 13.5 cm diameter
Purchased from the Jewish
Community of Malta, 1984-70 b,c

51
Torah shield
Lemberg (Lvov) (?), Poland, late 18th-
early 19th century
Silver, parcel-gilt, repoussé, agate and
carnelian stones, 31.7 × 21.6 cm
Gift of Dr Harry G. Friedman,
F 2280

50

51

52

52
Torah shield
Probably Rhodes, 1859/60
(inscription date)
Silver, openwork and engraved,
29.2 cm

Museum purchase: the Docents of
The Jewish Museum through the
Nash Aussenberg Memorial Fund,
1991-124

53
Torah shield
Hermannstadt, Hungary, 1778
Maker: Michael Gross (?) (master
1767-78)
Silver, cast, repoussé and appliqué,
32.4 × 19.7 cm
Gift of Mr B. W. Huebsch, JM 12-57

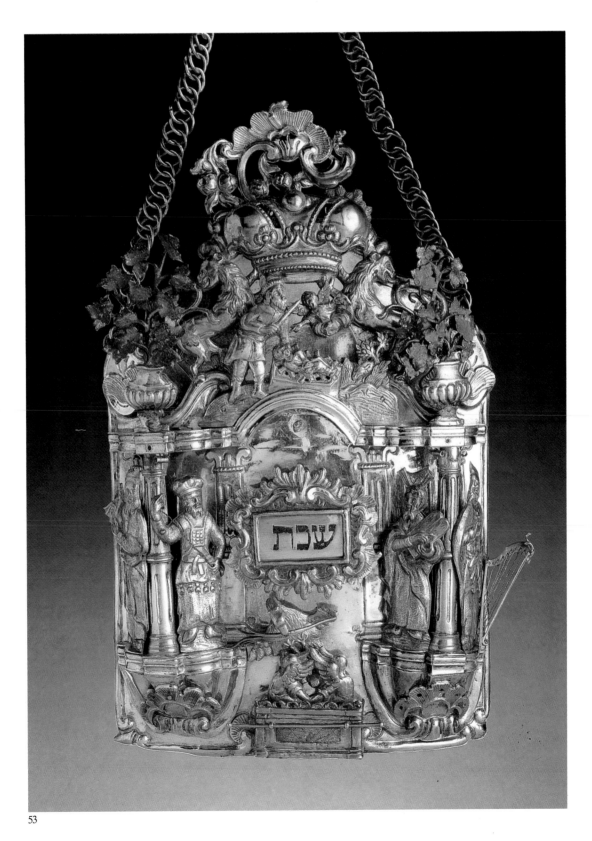

53

54
Torah case with finials (*tik* and *rimmonim*)
Paris, ca.1860
Maker: Maurice Mayer
Silver, cast, repoussé and parcel-gilt,
74.9 × 92.7 cm
Museum purchase from auction of
Benguiat collection, s 1456

55
Mantle for the Torah scroll
Amsterdam, 1771/72
Silk and metallic brocade; velvet,
embroidered with silk and metallic
threads
Oval top: 31.5 × 26 cm diameter
Body: 88 × 104 cm maximum width
The H. Ephraim and Mordecai
Benguiat Family Collection, s 18

54

56
Torah mantle with the Binding of Isaac
Pfaffenhofen, Alsace, 1875/76
Silk, embroidered with silk and metallic threads, spangles and stamped metal forms, 86.5 × 44.5 cm
Gift of Dr Harry G. Friedman in memory of Dr Murray Last, F 3546

57
Torah mantle
Galicia, 1870/71
Velvet, embroidered with beads and metallic threads, 64.5 × 40 cm
Gift of Dr Harry G. Friedman, F 3875

56

57

58
Torah binder
Florence (?), 1662/63
Maker: Rikah Polacco
Linen, embroidered with silk and
metallic threads, modern lining,
281.4 × 16.5 cm
Gift of Cora Ginsburg, 1988-21

59
Torah pointer
New York, 1984
Maker: Shirley Kagan
Silver, amethyst and ebony,
29 × 1.2 cm
Museum purchase, 1984-16

58

60
Torah binder
Schmalkalden, Germany, 1762
Linen, embroidered with silk thread,
18 × 348 cm
Gift of Dr Harry G. Friedman,
F 5096

61
Torah binder
Italy, early 17th century
Linen, embroidered with
multicolored silk threads,
19 × 325.1 cm
Gift of the Kadish Family, 1983-222

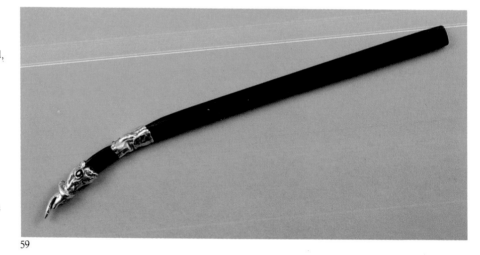

59

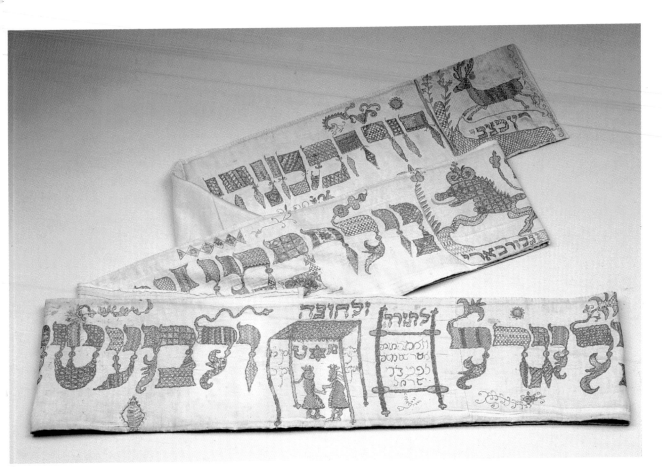

60

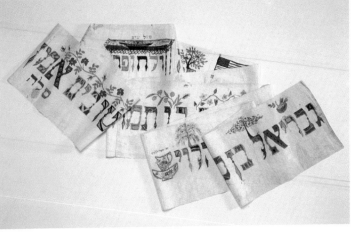

62

61

62
Torah binder
New York, 1869
Undyed linen, painted, 21.5 × 356 cm
Gift of Colonel George Feigel,
through Augusta and Harry Berger,
S 1070

63
Reader's desk cover
Mogilev, Belorussia, 1871
Maker: Johanan of Mogilev
Velvet embroidered with silk and
metallic threads, 106.9 × 142.1 cm
Gift of Mrs Rudnick, through Rabbi
Louis Epstein, s 1359

63

64
**Miniature reader's desk and
furnishings**

(a) Reader's desk
Danzig, 19th century
Wood; brass, cast, cut-out and
engraved; silver, engraved; velvet,
34.6 × 19.6 × 14.5 cm
Gift of the Danzig Jewish
Community, D 274

(b) Reader's desk cover
Germany (?), 18th century (fabric)
Silver and silver foil embroidered on
weave-patterned silk; metallic
sequins, 15.4 × 28 cm
Gift of the Danzig Jewish
Community, D 273

(c) Pair of candlesticks
Danzig (?), 19th century
Brass, cast, 8.9 × 4 cm
Gift of the Danzig Jewish
Community, D 104 a,b

65

65
Shiviti plaque
Prussia, 1803/4 (inscription date)
Brass, repoussé and gilt; ink on
parchment, 74.5 × 76.5 cm
Gift of the Danzig Jewish
Community, D 89

66
Plaque with Ten Commandments
Syria, late 19th century
Brass, inlaid with copper and silver,
47.6 × 33.7 cm
Judaica Acquisitions Fund, 1985-26

66

67

Memorial plaque and *omer* calendar of a society for the study of the mishnah (*ḥevrah mishnayyot*)
Rochester, New York, 1904
Artist: Barukh Zvi Ring (1870-1927)
Ink, gold and silver paint, colored pencil and watercolor on cut paper, 130.7 × 127 cm
Gift of Temple Beth Hamedresh-Beth Israel, Rochester, 1983-229

68

68
Shiviti **with topographic map of**
Israel
Istanbul, 1838/39
Artist: Moses Ganbash
Paint, ink and collage elements on
paper, 87 × 107.2 cm
Gift of Dr Harry G. Friedman, F 5855

69

69
Synagogue banner with prayer for King Wilhelm IV
Prussia, 1828
Paint on canvas, 112 × 70 cm
Gift of Dr Harry G. Friedman,
F 6026

70
Seven-branched candelabrum
Bauhaus, Weimar, 1922
Maker: Gyula Pap (Hungarian,
1899-1983)
Brass, 41.9 × 42.9 cm
Museum purchase: The Judaica
Endowment Acquisition Fund; Mrs
J. J. Wyle Gift, by exchange; The
Judaica Acquisitions Fund; The
Peter Cats Foundation; Helen and
Jack Cytryn; and Isaac Pollak,
1991-106

71
Bowl
Damascus, 1904/5
Brass, inlaid with silver, copper and
gold, 13.6 × 28.1 cm. diameter
Gift of Dr Harry G. Friedman, F 919

70

71

Tradition: The Jewish Year

The festivals of the Jewish year embody multiple layers of meaning. They mark the changing seasons, sanctifying time and expressing humankind's inherent relationship with the rhythms of nature. The seasonal festivals correspond to agricultural cycles and incorporate the memory of the Jews' history in Ancient Israel. Russian Jews celebrate the festival of spring, Passover, while snow is deep on the ground, and Jews living south of the equator commemorate the autumn harvest while spring is in full bloom. From antiquity on, the agricultural festivals were also associated with the most significant events in the history of the Jewish people: the Exodus from Egypt (Passover), the Giving of the Law at Sinai (Shavuot or the Feast of Weeks), the Wandering of the Israelites in the Desert (Sukkot or the Feast of Booths).

The triumphs and tragedies of Jewish history are commemorated with holidays such as Hanukkah and Purim. The first recalls the revolt of the Maccabees for religious freedom from Syria in 165BCE, and the second, the rescue of Persian Jewry from destruction in the 5th century BCE.

The most solemn days of the Jewish year, Rosh Hashanah (New Year) and Yom Kippur (the Day of Atonement), lack any agricultural or Jewish historical significance, and express more universal aspirations. Jews reflect on their actions during the past year as part of an effort to live an ethical life. As a call to repentance, a *shofar* or ram's horn is sounded one hundred times each day of the New Year's festival (fig. 77). It is also customary to send greetings to one's friends (figs. 73-76).

The first seasonal festival, Sukkot or the Feast of Booths, occurs just four days after the Day of Atonement. Observant Jews build booths (*sukkot*) representing the temporary homes inhabited by the ancient Israelites in the years between the Exodus from Egypt and their entry into the land of Canaan. During the holiday it is customary to eat in the *sukkah* (fig. 81). The Torah also commands that each Jew hold together four species of plants that grew in the land of Israel and recite blessings over them (fig. 79). They are the palm, the willow and the myrtle, which are bound together, and the citron, which is usually stored in a protective container (fig. 80).

In the winter month of Kislev, when Jewish patriots under the leadership of the Maccabees rebelled against their Greco-Syrian rulers and established religious and political freedom, they restored the Temple in Jerusalem. One of the objects replaced was the *menorah* or seven-branched lampstand. By the first centuries of this era, the holiday of Hannukah (whose name refers to the rededication of the Temple) was celebrated by the kindling of lights. The lamps used over the centuries have taken many forms, but all have eight lights, one for each day of the festival (figs. 82-92).

The second historical holiday of the Jewish calendar, Purim, falls in early spring, during the month of Adar. It is celebrated by reading the Story of Esther in the synagogue (fig. 94), by feasting (figs. 95 and 96), by exchanging gifts of food with friends and by giving alms to the poor.

Four weeks after Purim, Jews celebrate Passover, whose profound spiritual significance lies in its commemoration of the Israelites' attainment of physical and spiritual freedom after more than four hundred years of bondage in Egypt. Their experience as slaves, the process of emancipation and the Exodus are recalled by the recitation of the *Haggadah*, a compilation of prayers, historical narratives and hymns like the *Had Gadya* or *Tale of a Goat* (fig. 104), and by the eating of special foods at the Passover ritual meal, the *seder* (figs. 97-99, 101-103).

The third of the seasonal festivals falls seven weeks after the first day of Passover and is, therefore, called Shavuot (Weeks). The interval between the two holidays is marked by the ceremonial counting of the days between them, known as the 'counting of the *omer*', after the measure of barley brought each day to the Temple in Jerusalem (figs. 67 and 105). In Jewish tradition, the two holidays are linked by more than their calendrical relationship; Shavuot is regarded as the fulfilment of Passover. Only by accepting the moral and religious law of the Torah at Sinai did the Jewish people become spiritually free, completing the process of liberation begun at Passover with the Exodus from physical bondage in Egypt.

72
Rosh Hashanah plate
Delft, early 18th century
Maker: APK
Faience, 24.1 cm diameter
Gift of Mrs Theresa Goel, through
Dr Harry G. Friedman, F 2978

73
Casket with zodiac signs and other motifs: a New Year's gift
Germany, 15th-16th century, later additions
Fruitwood, carved and painted,
24 × 5.5 × 4.5 cm
Gift of Mr and Mrs Norman Zeiler
in memory of Mrs Nan Zeiler,
JM 35-66

72

73

74
Jewish New Year's greeting
Nome, Alaska, 1910
Attributed to Happy Jack (Inuit, ca.1870-1918)
Engraved walrus tusk with gold inset, 25.4 × 2.5 cm diameter
Gift of Kanofsky Family in memory of Minnie Kanofsky, 1984-71

75
Jewish New Year's greeting
Montreal, Quebec, ca.1932
Maker: Mordecai Cohen
Ink on paper, 51 × 53.2 cm
Gift of Abraham J. and Deborah B. Karp, 1987-141

76
Jewish New Year banner
United States, 1942/43
Undyed silk, printed, 43 × 32 cm
Gift of Mr Vaxer through Dr Harry G. Friedman, F 6025

74

75

76

77
Shofar
Ethiopia (?), 19th century
Ram's horn, coral, 62.9 cm long
Gift of Dr Harry G. Friedman, F 5280

78
Commemorative panel
depicting Jewish soldiers observing
the Day of Atonement in a
German army camp at Metz
Germany, 1870
Undyed cotton, printed in red and
black, 65 × 67 cm
Gift of Dr Harry G. Friedman, F 4364

77

78

79

80

81

82

79
Leopold Pilichowski
(Polish, 1869-1933)
Sukkoth, 1894-95
Oil on canvas, 108 × 134.6 cm
Gift of Mr and Mrs Oscar Gruss,
JM 89-55

80
Etrog **container**
Augsburg, ca.1670-80
Maker: KB
Silver, gilt, hammered and chased,
19.1 × 23 cm
Gift of Dr Harry G. Friedman,
F 4390

81
Solomon Joseph Solomon
(British, 1860-1927)
High Tea in the Sukkah, 1906
Ink, graphite and gouache on paper,
39.4 × 29.2 cm
Gift of Edward J. Sovatkin, JM 91-55

82
Hanukkah lamp
Frankfurt-am-Main, ca.1680
Maker: Johann Valentin Schüler
(1650-1720)
Silver, gilt, 25.1 × 31.1 × 7 cm
Gift of Norman S. Goetz, Henry
A. Loeb, Henry L. Marx, Ira
A. Schur, Lawrence A. Wien,
Leonard Block, Gustave L. Levy,
Robert I. Wischnick, JM 19-64

83

84

83
Hanukkah lamp with figure of Judith
Italy, 16th-17th century
Brass, cast, 21 × 22.2 × 5.7 cm
Gift of Dr Harry G. Friedman, F 129

85

84
Hanukkah lamp
The Hague, ca.1750
Maker: Reymer de Haan (?)
Silver, cast, chased and repoussé,
30.5 × 24.3 × 5.7 cm
Gift of Dr Harry G. Friedman, F 3693

85
Hanukkah lamp
Frankfurt-am-Main, 1706-32
Maker: Johann Adam Boller
(1679-1732)
Silver, cast, engraved, cut-out and gilt,
44.2 × 38.7 × 24.2 cm
Gift from the Estate of Alice
B. Goldschmidt, 1983-160

86
**Hanukkah lamp in the form of a
Torah ark**
Brody, 1787
Maker: BZK
Silver, cast, repoussé, appliqué,
openwork, chased, cut-out, and
parcel-gilt, 69.8 × 44.1 cm
The H. Ephraim and Mordecai
Benguiat Family Collection, s 260

86

87
Hanukkah lamp with lions
Jerusalem, ca.1930
Bezalel School
Brass, hammered, embossed and
punched, 14 × 13 × 6.1 cm
Gift of Dr Harry G. Friedman, F 1309

88
**Hanukkah lamp with American
eagle**
United States, ca.1900
Tin, cast and brass-plated,
41.6 × 40 × 16.5 cm
Gift of Dr Harry G. Friedman in
memory of Prof. Israel Davidson,
F 1589

87

88

89

89
Hanukkah lamp
North Africa, 19th-20th century
Brass, cast, cut-out and engraved,
34 × 27.9 cm
Gift of Dr Harry G. Friedman, F 4161

90

90
Hanukkah lamp
Princeton, New Jersey, 1974
Maker: Mae Shafter Rockland
(b.1937)
Wood covered in fabric with molded
plastic figures, 27.9 × 60.9 × 17.8 cm
Gift of the artist, 1984-127 a,b

91
Hanukkah lamp # 7
Los Angeles, 1986
Maker: Peter Shire
Painted steel, anodized aluminum,
chrome, 54 × 57.1 × 43.2 cm
Judaica Acquisitions Endowment
Fund, 1989-20

92
Hanukkah lamp
Leveroy, Holland, 1988
Maker: Eduard Hermans
Stoneware, 23.6 × 42 cm
Judaica Acquisitions Fund, 1989-67

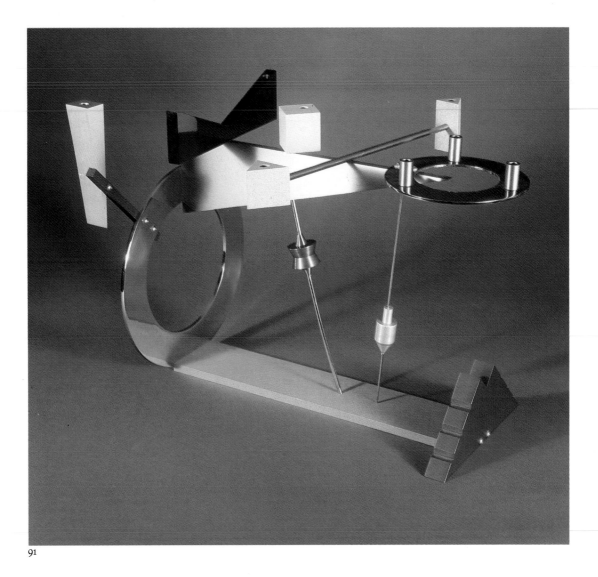

91

92

93
Purim wall decoration
Jerusalem, late 19th century
Maker: Sara Eydel Weissburg
Perforated paper embroidered with
wool and silk, 67 × 53 cm
Gift of Mrs Pearl Schwartz, S 1337

94
Scroll of Esther
Amsterdam, after 1641
Engraver: Salom Italia
(1619-after 1655)
Parchment, engraved and
manuscript, 20 × 250.5 cm
Gift of the Danzig Jewish
Community, D 76

93

94

95
Purim Wall Decoration
Vienna, 1929
Maker: Maier Schwartz
Printed on paper, mounted on
cardboard, 35.9 × 45.7 cm
Gift of Dr Harry G. Friedman, F 4308

96
**Purim beaker with celebratory
figures**
Augsburg, ca.1690
Silver, engraved and parcel-gilt,
5.6 × 5 cm
Gift of Richard Scheuer, 1981-6

95

Purim Wall Decoration

96

73

97

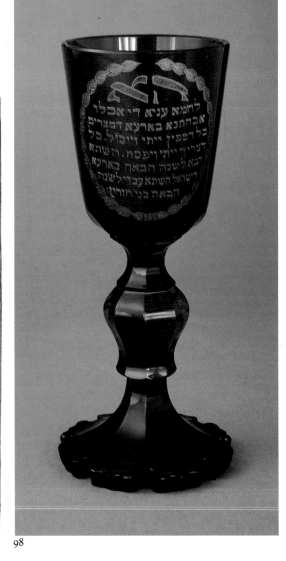

98

97
Meichel Pressman
(American, 1864-1953)
The Seder, 1950
Watercolor on paper, 56.5 × 47 cm
Gift of Dr Henry Pressman, JM 10-53

98
Passover goblet inscribed with
ha laḥma
Bohemia, 3rd quarter 19th century
Glass, free-blown, tooled, ruby-
flashed and wheel-engraved,
21.5 × 8.7 cm
Gift of Dr Harry G. Friedman,
F 4907

99

101

99
Seder plate
Vienna, ca.1900
Maker: LQR
Ceramic, glazed; 37.5 cm diameter
Gift of A. Benedict Doran, 1984-49

100
Passover banner
Possibly Alsace, 1828/29
Linen, painted; open weave, knotted
cotton fringe, 141 × 41.5 cm
Gift of Dr Harry G. Friedman,
F 5004

101
Matzah bag
Germany, 19th century
Maker: SN
Undyed silk/cotton satin,
embroidered with polychrome silk,
38.5 × 40.5 cm
Gift of Dr and Mrs Max Gottschalk,
JM 47-59

100

Tiered *seder* set
Poland, 18th-19th century
Brass, cast, cut-out and engraved;
wood, painted and stained; ink on
paper; silk, embroidered; linen;
cotton, 35 × 35.5 cm diameter
Gift of the Danzig Jewish
Community, D 115

102

103
Tiered *seder* set
Frankfurt-am-Main, 1930
Maker: Ludwig Wolpert (1900-81)
Silver, ebony and glass
25.4 high × 40.6 diameter
Promised gift of Sylvia Zenia
Wiener

103

104
El Lissitzky
(Russian, 1890-1941)
The Fire Came and Burnt the Stick,
from *Ḥad Gadya (Tale of a Goat)*, 1919

Color lithograph on paper,
27.3 × 25.4 cm
Gift of Leonard and Phyllis
Greenberg, 1986-121g

105

***Omer* calendar**
Jerusalem, 1984
Maker: Georges Goldstein
Wool, 78.7 × 76.2 cm
Morris and Eva Feld Judaica
Acquisitions Fund, 1984-92

105

Tradition: The Sabbath

'More than Israel has preserved the Sabbath, the Sabbath has preserved Israel.' (Aḥad ha-Am, 1856-1927)

Observance of Shabbat (the Sabbath) distinguished the Israelites from other ancient peoples and introduced the revolutionary idea of granting everyone, including servants and domestic animals, one day of rest in every seven. This day of rest is one of Judaism's great legacies, for the concept was adopted by Christianity and Islam. Yet the Jewish observance of Shabbat remains one of the chief distinctions between Jews and their neighbors.

Shabbat commemorates God's rest after creation. Observant Jews refrain from categories of work such as igniting flames, washing clothes or baking between sunset on Friday and an hour after sunset on Saturday. Members of the community seek spiritual renewal through prayer, study of the Torah, and festive family meals accompanied by songs and blessings (figs. 106, 109, 111, 114).

Jews celebrate Shabbat to create a sense of sacred time. Its rituals separate it from the rest of the week, beginning with the kindling of lights (figs. 107 and 108) and a benediction over wine (fig. 110), and ending with the *havdalah* (separation) ceremony, whose similar elements inaugurate the new week (figs. 112 and 113).

106

106
Isidor Kaufmann
(Austrian, 1853-1921)
Friday Evening, ca.1920
Oil on canvas, 72.4 × 90.2 cm
Gift of Mr and Mrs
M. R. Schweitzer, JM 4-63

107

107
Pair of candlesticks
Russia, late 18th century
Silver, cast, incised and stippled,
17.1 × 7.9 cm
Gift of Mrs Miriam Miller,
1985-170 a,b

108
**Hanging lamp for Sabbath and
festivals**
Frankfurt-am-Main, 1680-1720
Maker: Johann Valentin Schüler
(1650-1720)
Silver, cast, repoussé and engraved,
56.5 × 36.8 cm diameter
Jewish Cultural Reconstruction,
JM 37-52

108

109
Sabbath cloth
Iran, 1806
Cotton, embroidered with
polychrome silk, 83 cm diameter
Gift of Dr Harry G. Friedman,
F 4007

110
Kiddush **beakers**

(a) **Moscow,** 1739-63
Maker: Andrej Gerasimow
Silver, repoussé and engraved,
5.1 × 5.4 cm
The Rose and Benjamin Mintz
Collection, M 227

(b) **Russia,** 18th century
Silver, repoussé, parcel-gilt, chased
and engraved, 9.2 × 7.5 cm
The Rose and Benjamin Mintz
Collection, M 230

(c) **Moscow,** 1768
Maker: Peter Semenov (master
1739-77)
Silver, engraved, cast and parcel-gilt,
5 × 6.1 cm
The Rose and Benjamin Mintz
Collection, M 229

(d) **Nuremberg,** 1675-1700
Silver, parcel-gilt, repoussé, chased,
engraved and cast, 9.5 × 8.3 cm
Gift of Herbert Gutmann in memory
of Herman Gutmann (1856-1905),
JM 18-50

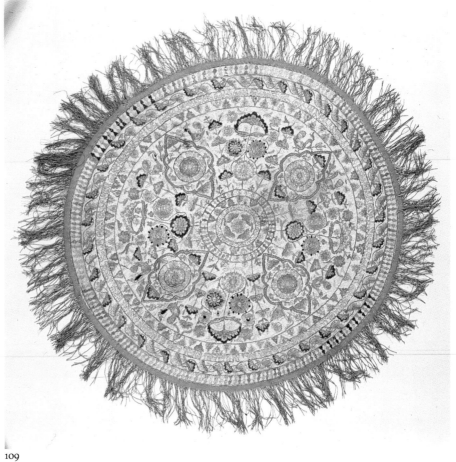

109

110

ברוך אתה יי אלהינו מלך העולם הזן
את העולם כלו בטובו בחן בחסד
וברחמים הוא נתן לחם לכל בשר כי
לעולם חסדו ובטובו הגדול תמיד לא
חסר לנו ואל יחסר לנו מזון לעולם ועד
בעבור שמו הגדול כי הוא זן ומפרנס
לכל ומטיב לכל ומכן מזון לכל בריותיו
אשר ברא כדכר אתה יי הזן את הכל ס
ואל תצריכנו יי אלהינו לא לידי
מתנת בשר ודם ולא לידי הלואתם כ
אם לידך המלאה הפתוחה הקדושה
והרחבה שלא נבוש ולא נכלם לעולם
ועד הרחמן הוא ימלוך עלינו לעולם
ועד הרחמן הוא יתברך בשמים
ובארץ הרחמן הוא פרנסנו בכבוד
עשה שלום במרומיו...אשה
שלום עלינו ועל כל ישראל אמן

111

111
Wall hanging with *Grace after Meals*
Offenbach, Germany, 1925
Maker: Berthold Wolpe (British,
b. Germany, 1905)
Workshop of Rudolf Koch (German,
1876-1934)
Undyed hand-woven linen,
embroidered with dyed linen,
271 × 145 cm
Gift of Milton Rubin, JM 33-48

112
Spice container
Poland, 1810-20
Silver, repoussé, cast, engraved,
filigree, chased and parcel-gilt,
50.8 cm high
The H. Ephraim and Mordecai
Benguiat Family Collection, JM 34-51

113
***Havdalah* candlestick and spice
container**
Mühlhausen, 1819-38
Maker: Risier
Silver, embossed and chased,
22.8 cm high × 9.5 cm diameter
Gift of Mr and Mrs Jean Paul Latil,
1982-61

114
Cooking pot
Frankfurt-am-Main, 1579/80
Brass, cast, chased and hammered,
21.2 cm high × 22.8 cm diameter
Gift of Mr and Mrs Ben Heller,
JM 23-64

112

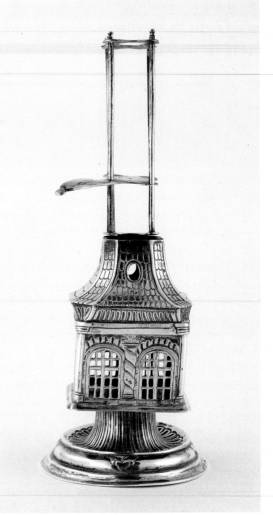

113

114

Tradition: The Life Cycle and Daily Life

Like all peoples, Jews have evolved ceremonies to mark major events in the life of a human being: birth, coming of age, marriage and death. These traditional rituals emphasize the link between the individual Jew and the larger community. A baby is given its name in the presence of the community or its representatives. The naming of a male child occurs at the conclusion of circumcision on the eighth day of life, a rite marking the child's entry into the covenant between God and Israel (figs. 115, 116, 118). The passage to adulthood, to personal responsibility for the commandments of the Torah, is celebrated by the young person's reading of a portion of the biblical text during synagogue services. At their marriage, a bride and groom symbolically establish a new household in Israel. A central part of the ceremony is the writing and transferral of a *ketubbah* or contract specifying the obligations of bride and groom (figs. 119 and 120). At the end of life, the deceased is prepared for burial by members of the communal Burial Society (figs. 127, 129).

For the observant Jew, each day is filled with practices that affirm Jewish identity and link the individual to the divine. Most of these acts are rooted in the Torah or the Talmud, while others are examples of folk religion. The placement of a *mezuzah*, a scroll inscribed with passages from Deuteronomy set within a protective case, on the doorpost of the home is an example of adherence to a biblical injunction (figs. 130, 131), while the wearing of amulets is a folk practice (fig. 117).

The daily order of prayers, for the morning, afternoon and evening are ascribed to the Patriarchs Abraham, Isaac and Jacob, suggesting the antiquity of this form of worship. During morning services, worshippers wear leather boxes containing biblical passages on their heads and arms, literally adhering to the command 'Bind them as a sign upon your hand and as a symbol on your foreheads' (Deut. 6:8 and 11:12; figs. 135-36). Where appropriate, worshippers face eastward toward Jerusalem, a direction often marked by a decorative plaque on the wall (figs. 132 and 133).

The Museum also collects works of historical importance or works used in the secular realm of daily life by Jews. Uriah Phillips Levy (1792-1862), for example, was a notable officer in the United States Navy who led the campaign to abolish flogging as a form of punishment. He was also an early preservationist, rescuing Monticello and its furnishings from ruin after Thomas Jefferson's death. The ceremonial cane presented to Levy upon his retirement from the Navy is now part of the Museum's collection (fig. 138).

115
Cushion cover for the circumcision ceremony
Austrian Empire, 1779/80
Silk velvet, embroidered with silk and metallic threads, 72.4 × 67.3 cm
Gift of Dr S. A. Buchenholz, s 1015

115

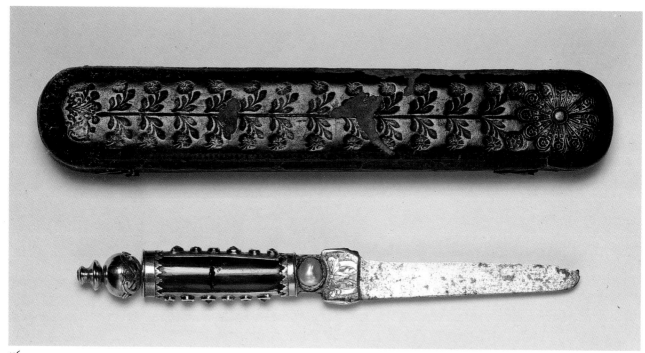

116

116
Circumcision knife and case
Germany, ca.1720
Silver, parcel-gilt, amber, garnets,
pearls
Case: leather, 19.1 cm high
Gift of Dr Harry G. Friedman,
F 2206

117
Amulet
Rome, 1809-10
Maker: Vincenzo Parenti (1767-1819)
Silver, cast, openwork and engraved,
12.4 × 6 cm
Gift of Abraham Bornstein, JM 16-51

117

118

**Torah curtain for the circumcision
ceremony**
Mannheim, 1728/29
Silk and velvet, embroidered with
polychrome and metallic threads,
190.5 × 143.5 cm
Gift of Rose Weinfeld, JM 4-49

118

119

Marriage contract of Shimshon, son of Kalonymous Ha-Levi and Grazia, daughter of Asher Fano
Trieste, Italy, 1774
Ink on parchment, cut out,
70.5 × 56.5 cm
Gift of Dr Harry G. Friedman, F 5355

120

Marriage contract of Baba called Mattiya, son of Isaac Muruti, and Hannah, daughter of Elihu Kashi
Iran, 1871
Ink, gouache and gold paint on paper, 76.2 × 50.2 cm
Gift of Amanollah Rokhsar,
1982-240

121

Coffee service
Staffordshire, England, 1769
Salt-glazed stoneware, painted with overglaze polychrome enamels
Tray, 33 cm diameter; coffee pot,
21.3 × 18.4 cm; pitcher, 12.7 × 10.2 cm;
waste bowl, 6.3 × 14.3 cm; sugar bowl,
8.2 × 10 cm diameter
Gift of the Felix M. and Frieda
Schiff Warburg Foundation,
JM 26-59 a-e

119

120

Double marriage cup
Augsburg, ca.1650-60
Maker: Hans Jakob Wild II
(1650-1733)
Silver, engraved, repoussé and parcel-
gilt, 14.7 × 6.2 cm
Gift of Harry G. Friedman, F 2587 a,b

121

122

123

123
Wedding sofa
Northern Germany, possibly Danzig,
1838
Birch veneer over pine; lindenwood,
painted and gilt, upholstered,
97 × 160 × 71 cm
Gift of the Danzig Jewish
Community, D 280

124
Presentation plate
Prague, 1786
Maker: Joseph Mitterbacher
Pewter, engraved, 27.9 × 32.4 cm
Gift of Mrs Atlas, 1983-227

125
Presentation urn
Copenhagen, ca.1880-85
Maker: Bing and Grøndahl
Ceramic, painted, 22.2 cm high
Gift of Mr and Mrs Asher
Rosenberg, 1983-231

124

125

126

126
**Hakham and widow in the
Cemetery of Pera, Constantinople,**
from Amadeo Preziosi, *Stamboul,
Souvenir d'Orient*
Paris, 1865
Colored lithograph on paper,
41.2 × 31.2 cm
Gift of Dr Harry G. Friedman, F 5885

127
**Left: Beaker of the Burial Society
of Worms**
Nuremberg, 1711/12 (inscription date)
Maker: Johann Conrad Weiss
(active 1699-1751)
Silver, parcel-gilt, engraved,
24.8 × 12.5 cm
Gift of Michael Oppenheim, Mainz,
JM 30-51

**Right: Beaker of the Burial Society
of Worms**
Possibly Worms, ca.1732
Silver, hammered and engraved,
24.8 × 13 cm
Gift of Michael Oppenheim, Mainz,
JM 31—51

127

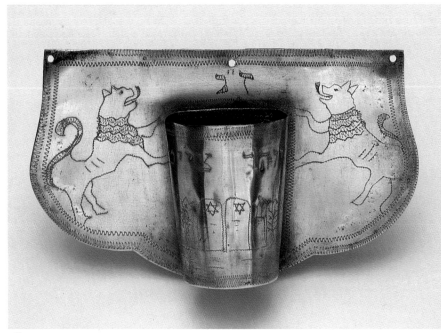

128

128
Memorial (*yahrzeit*) sconce
Probably Russia, late 19th - 20th
century
Maker: VIP
Silver, engraved, 11.3 × 19.3 × 7.3 cm
Gift of Dr Harry G. Friedman, F 3429

129
Beaker of the Polin Burial Society
Bohemia, 1691
Glass, enameled, 24.4 × 13.1 cm
Gift of Dr Harry G. Friedman, F 3211

129

130
Mezuzah
Galicia, ca.1850
Wood, carved; ink on parchment,
26.5 × 5.7 cm
Gift of Dr Harry G. Friedman, F 3189

131
Beron *mezuzah*
New York, 1991
Maker: Harley Swedler (b. 1962)
Bronze, cast with a patina finish;
sterling silver, stainless steel and
rolled glass, 11.4 × 5.7 cm
Gift of Edna S. Beron and Harley
Swedler, 1992-31

132
Decoration for the eastern wall
(*Mizraḥ*)
Alsace, ca.1800
Reverse painting on glass,
43.2 × 45.1 cm
The Jewish Museum, s 1461

133
Decoration for the eastern wall
(*Mizraḥ*)
Pitcomen, Austria
Artist: Israel Dov Rosenbaum
Paint, ink and pencil on cut-out
paper, 91.4 × 61 cm
Gift of Helen W. Finkel in memory
of Israel Dov Rosenbaum, Bessie
Rosenbaum Finkel and Sidney
Finkel, 1987-136

130

131

132

133

134
Prayer shawl
Probably Russia, late 19th century
Silk, hand-embroidered with silk
threads, 243.8 × 70.5 cm
Gift of Jerome and Miriam Katzin
in memory of Dr Louis Finkelstein,
1991-48

135

134

136

135
***Tefillin* bag of the Levi family**
Italy, 18th century
Silk, embroidered with silk and
metallic threads, 34 × 25.4 cm
Gift of Paola Soria Sereni, 1990-39

136
Cases for *tefillin*
New York, 1963
Maker: Moshe Zabari (b.1935)
Silver, pierced; ebony, 6.4 × 14 cm
Gift of the Abram and Frances
Kanof Collection of Contemporary
Jewish Ceremonial Art, JM 72-65 a,b

137
Purse of Abraham Cohen (d.1793)
United States, 1766
Wool, petit point; silk taffeta,
24.1 × 22.2 cm
Judaica Acquisitions Fund, 1985-31

138
Cane presented to Uriah P. Levy
United States, dated 1860
Whalebone; ivory, carved and
stained, 86 × 3.7 cm
Eva and Morris Feld Judaica
Acquisitions Fund, Daniel M.
Friedenberg, Jack Tepper, Mildred
and George Weissman, Isaac Pollak,
Kurt Thalberg, 1990-7

137

138

Confronting Modernity:
1700-1948

For over a thousand years, traditional boundaries, both within the community and without, limited Jews' roles in society, their opportunities and their rights. A minority everywhere, Jews were usually granted some communal self-government, but were restricted in where they could live, the occupations they could pursue, and the legal and civic rights they enjoyed. In most countries, only a privileged few escaped these restrictions.

In the modern world, Jewish life was dramatically transformed by the eighteenth-century philosophy of the Enlightenment. The concepts of liberty, equality and the improvement of humankind through education and historical progress spread throughout Europe, sparking a new attitude towards Jews and a reconsideration of their status.

One of the areas of endeavor now open to Jews was the arts. For centuries, élite training had depended on the Christian guild system and later on art schools, which were closed to Jews. In the modern world, arts education became secularized, with the result that Jews ceased to be merely sitters (figs. 139-140), and became themselves sculptors and painters, often moving to the great centers like Paris to learn from other artists and from the art of the museums (figs. 145, 147-150). Jewish artists took part in the great experiments of modernism. At the end of this period, their works began to encompass the two most awesome events of Jewish life in the modern era, the *Shoah* or destruction of European Jewry by the Nazis (fig. 154) and the establishment of a Jewish homeland in Israel (fig. 153).

Thomas Sully
(American, 1783-1872)
Portrait of Sally Etting, 1808
Oil on canvas, 76.2 × 63.5 cm
Gift of William Wollman
Foundation, F 4610

140
**August Amant Constant Fidèle
Edouart** (French, 1789-1861)
Silhouettes of the Kursheedt Family,
1840
Cut paper, 31.1 × 38.1 cm
Gift of Dr Harry G. Friedman, F 3883

139

140

141
Moritz Daniel Oppenheim
(German, 1800-82)
*The Return of the Jewish Volunteer
from the Wars of Liberation to his
Family still Living in Accordance with
Old Customs*, 1833-34
Oil on canvas, 86.4 × 91.4 cm
Gift of Mr and Mrs Richard D. Levy
with donor maintaining life estate,
1984-61

142
Maurycy Minkowski
(Polish, 1881-1930)
He Cast à Look and Was Hurt, 1910
Oil on canvas, 73.6 × 106.6 cm
Gift of Mrs Rose Mintz, JM 14-75

141

142

143

143
Samuel Hirszenberg
(Polish, 1865-1908)
The Black Banner, 1905
Oil on canvas, 76.2 × 205.7 cm
Gift of the Estate of Rose Mintz,
JM 63-67

144
Abraham Manievich
(American, b. Russia, 1882/83-1942)
Destruction of the Ghetto, Kiev, 1919
Oil on canvas, 198.1 × 188 cm
Gift of Mrs Leslie Bezark in memory
of her husband, 1991-30

145
Marc Chagall
(French, b. Vitebsk, 1887-1985)
Man and the Village, ca.1914
Oil on canvas, 58.4 × 48.3 cm
Promised Gift of Frances Gershwin
Godowsky and Family in memory
of George Gershwin

144

146

146
Jacob Epstein
(British, b. New York, 1880-1959)
A Hester Street Crowd, ca.1900-02
Black crayon on paper,
60.3 × 25.8 cm
Gift of Karl Nathan, JM 11-51

147
Elie Nadelman
(American, b. Warsaw, 1882-1946)
Dancer, ca.1918-19
Cherrywood, 71.8 cm high
Given in memory of Muriel Rand by
her husband William Rand, 1992-37

147

148
Chaim Soutine
(Lithuanian, 1893-1943)
Bell Boy, ca.1928
Oil on canvas, 66 × 50.8 cm
Promised Gift; The Muriel and
William Rand Collection

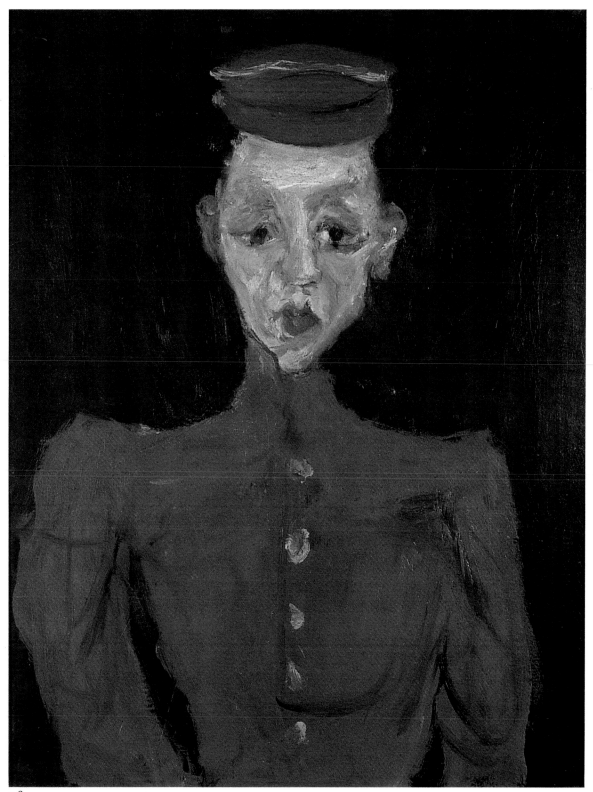

148

Max Weber
(American, b. Russia, 1881-1969)
The Talmudists, 1934
Oil on canvas, 127 × 85.7 cm
Gift of Mrs Nathan Miller, JM 51-48

150
Chana Orloff
(French, 1888-1968)
Madame B.S. [Blocq-Serruys], 1927
Plaster, 34.3 cm high
Gift of Enia Alter Propp, 1986-154

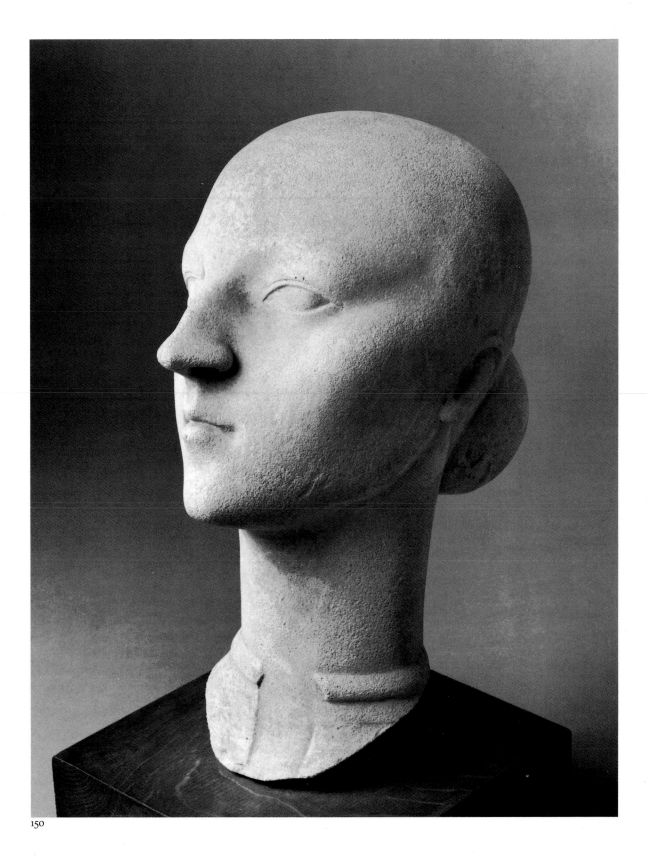

150

151

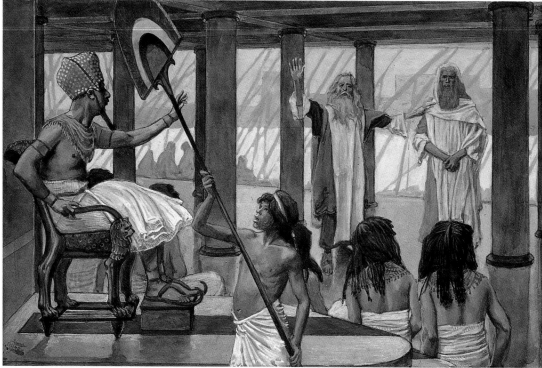

152

153

151
La Maison Bonfils
(French firm, active 1867-ca.1907)
The Western Wall, 1867-ca.1907
Albumen print, 22.4 × 28.3 cm
JM 89-68

152
James Jacques Joseph Tissot
(French, 1836-1902)
Joseph Dwelleth in Egypt, ca.1896-1902
Gouache on board, 23.2 × 27.7 cm
Gift of the Heirs of Jacob H. Schiff,
X 1952-141

153
Reuven Rubin
(Israeli, b. Romania, 1893-1974)
Goldfish Vendor, 1928
Oil on canvas, 74.9 × 61 cm
Gift of Kitty and Harold
J. Ruttenberg, 1985-227

Realizing a Future:
The Contemporary World
(1948)

In the passage from Traditional Worlds to Modernity, Jews emerged from an age in which identity depended on the community, to one in which identity is formed by the individual. Free to choose which elements define their Jewishness, some have chosen nationalism centered on the State of Israel; others have transferred the Jewish sense of responsibility for the community to broader social movements; a portion of the Jewish community has remained committed to religious observance, while others have transformed the Jewish imperative to study religious texts into a commitment to scholarship of a general type. These are only a few of the contemporary responses to the issue of Jewish identity.

Israeli artists face even more complex problems of identity. They are members of international artistic movements, but as citizens of a country always at war, that was born in the aftermath of the Holocaust, they face critical issues of security and its consequences for the contemporary population (figs. 156-158). Some express the problems of the Holocaust, a theme shared with Jewish artists elsewhere (figs. 163 and 170), while others create works on the social tensions of contemporary Israeli society.

In the last few years, some artists have turned to traditional themes as part of a search for Jewish identity: to the legendary Golem (fig. 175), Jewish ritual (fig. 172), scenes of past Jewish life (fig. 165) and to autobiographical explorations. This phenomenon may be linked to a general American development, a belief in the validity of multiculturism.

As each of these developments unfolds, The Jewish Museum considers and presents them in its exhibitions and permanently records them in its acquisitions. The Museum's collections continue to be a mirror of Jewish history, Jewish culture and philosophical concerns as reflected in the art of the present and the future.

154
Lasar Segall
(Brazilian, b. Lithuania, 1891-1957)
Exodus, 1947
Oil on canvas, 132 × 137.1 cm
Gift of James Rosenberg and George
Baker in memory of Felix
M. Warburg, JM 25-48

155
Rico Lebrun
(American, b. Italy, 1900-64)
Study for Dachau Chamber, 1958
Oil on canvas, 200.7 × 215.9 cm
Gift of Constance Lebrun Crown,
1986-225

154

155

156
Joshua Neustein
(Israeli, b. Danzig, 1940)
Weimar Series II, 1981
Paper and acrylic construction,
188.6 × 147.6 cm
Gift of Selma and Stanley I. Batkin,
1981-241

156

157
Menashe Kadishman
(Israeli, b. 1932)
Shepherdess, 1984
Acrylic on canvas, 179.1 × 156.2 cm
Gift of Fred Stein, 1987-84

158
Moshe Gershuni
(Israeli, b.1936)
Where is My Soldier?, 1981
Glass paint, oil stick and lacquer on
paper, 70 × 100 cm
Museum purchase, 1984-24

157

158

159
Joshua Borkovsky
(Israeli, b.1952)
Ship/Map (No. 1), 1990
Diptych, tempera and oil on wood
panel, 80 × 45 cm
Museum purchase; Gift of the
Ariana and Jack Weintraub
Foundation for the Arts, 1991-43

160
Michael Gross
(Israeli, b.1920)
Self-Portrait, 1983
Oil on canvas, 195.3 × 96.5 cm
Museum purchase, through funds
provided by Blanche and Romie
Shapiro, 1990-155

159

160

161

Deganit Berest
(Israeli, b.1949)
After Dialectica and 'Brownian Motion',
1988
Oil on canvas, 165 × 218 cm
Museum purchase; Gift of the
Ariana and Jack Weintraub
Foundation for the Arts, 1990-143

162

Moshe Kupferman
(Israeli, b. Galicia, 1926)
Untitled, 1974
Oil on canvas, 129.5 × 157.8 cm
Gift of Nitza Etra, 1984-57

162

163

163
George Segal
(American, b.1924)
The Holocaust, 1982
Plaster, wood and wire,
304.8 × 609.6 × 609.6 cm
Museum purchase, through funds
provided by the Dorot Foundation,
1985-176a-l

164
Torah curtain
Millburn, New Jersey, 1950-51
Designer: Adolph Gottlieb
(American, 1903-74)
Produced by the women of
Congregation Bnai Israel, Millburn,
New Jersey, under the supervision of
Esther Gottlieb
Velvet, appliquéd, embroidered with
metallic thread
Upper section: 204.5 × 286.4 cm
Lower section: 207 × 309.2 cm
Gift of Congregation Bnai Israel,
Millburn, New Jersey, 1987-23a–d

165

164

165
R. B. Kitaj
(British, b.1932)
*Study for the Jewish School
(Joe Singer as a Boy)*, 1980
Pastel and charcoal on paper,
77.5 × 56.5 cm
Museum purchase, through funds
provided by the Abraham
A. Mitchell Charitable Foundation,
the Joshua Lowenfish Bequest and
an Anonymous Gift, 1986-209

166
Hannah Wilke
(American, 1940-93)
Seura Chaya #1, 1978-89
Photograph and watercolor,
149.9 × 160 cm
Gift of Donald Goddard, 1991-44

167
Brian Weil
(American, b.1954)
Untitled (Young Man), 1985
From the series 'Hasidim'
Black-and-white photograph,
79.7 × 53 cm
Museum purchase; Albert A. List
Gift and Rictavia Schiff Bequest, by
exchange, 1991-112

168
Larry Rivers
(American, b.1925)
Portrait of Vera List, ca.1965
Wood, paint, glass and aluminum,
81.3 × 68.6 cm
Gift of Vera G. List, 1984-21

169
Larry Sultan
(American, b.1946)
Untitled (My Mother Posing for Me),
1984
From the series 'Pictures from
Home'
Ektacolor Plus print, 72.1 × 87.3 cm
Museum purchase; Ferkauf Fund,
1991-110

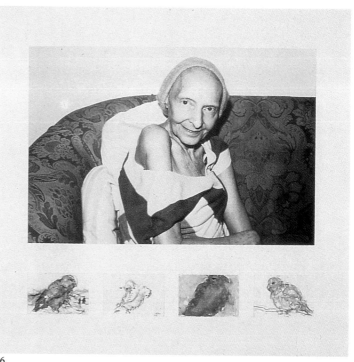

166

167

168

169

170

171

170
Leonard Baskin
(American, b.1922)
The Altar, 1977
Carved, laminated lindenwood,
152.4 × 180.3 × 91.4 cm
Gift of Mr Herman Tenenbaum and
the Saul and Suzanne Mutterperl
Bequest, by exchange, in honor of
Mildred and George Weissman,
1984-142

171
Alain Kirili
(French, b.1946)
Commandment II, 1980
Forged iron, 17 elements,
approximately 37 cm high
Museum purchase, through funds
provided by Vera G. and Albert
A. List, and Hyman L. and Joan
C. Sall, 1984-137

172

172
Louise Fishman
(American, b.1939)
Tashlich, 1984
Oil on linen, 64.1 × 43.8 cm
Gift of the artist in memory of
Kristie A. Jayne, 1990-5

173

173
Irving Petlin
(American, b.1934)
Street in Weissewald, 1986-87
Oil on canvas, 158.1 × 190.8 cm
Museum purchase, through funds
provided by S. H. and Helen
R. Scheuer Family Foundation,
1987-100

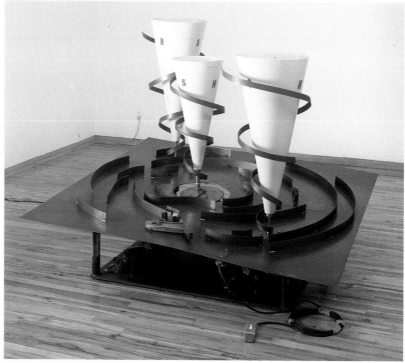

174

174
Alice Aycock
(American, b.1946)
Greased Lightning, 1984
Steel, motors and theatrical lighting,
142.2 × 182.8 × 182.8 cm
Museum purchase, through funds
provided by Miriam R. Passerman,
Louise and Gabriel Rosenfeld, and
Steven and Harriet Passerman in
memory of Maxwell W. Passerman,
1989-80

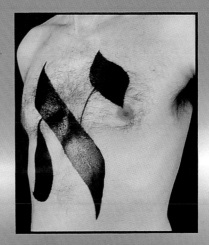

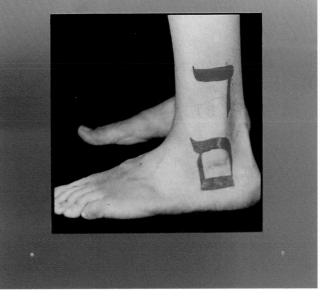

175
Gerlovina, Berghash, Gerlovin
(Rimma Gerlovina, Russian, b.1951;
Mark Berghash, American, b.1935;
Valeriy Gerlovin, Russian, b.1945)
Golem II, 1987
Four segments of coupler color
prints, framed in brushed aluminum,
182.8 × 129.5 cm
Museum purchase, through funds
provided by Elizabeth Cats, 1990-2   175

176

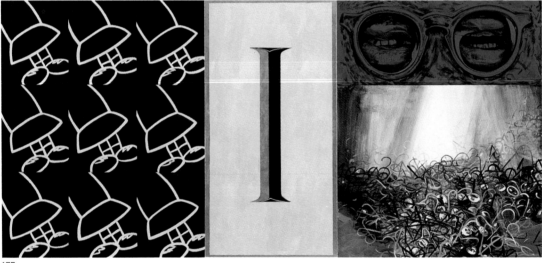

177

176
Wallace Berman
(American, 1926-76)
Untitled, 1972
Stones, paint, wood, screws and glass,
24.1 × 34.3 × 16.5 cm
Museum purchase; The Joshua
Lowenfish Bequest, 1987-109

177
Deborah Kass
(American, b.1952)
Subject Matters, 1989-90
Enamel, gold leaf and acrylic on
canvas
Two panels, 160 × 342.9 cm
Museum purchase, with funds
provided by Barbara S. Horowitz
and Joan C. Sall, 1992-38

178
William Anastasi
(American, b.1933)
Untitled, 1987
Oil on canvas, 325.1 × 325.1 cm
Gift of the artist, 1987-115a-d

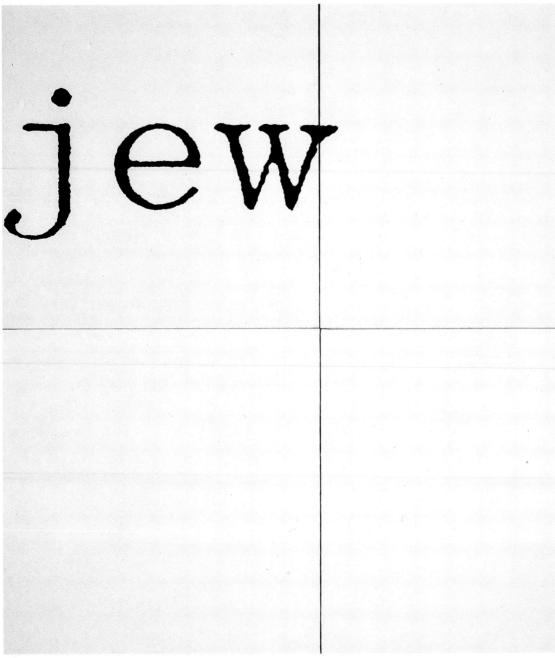

178

Index

Alder, Cyrus 8, 12, 19
Africa, North 45, 46, 69
Alsace 50, 75, 96
Anastasi, William 127
Augsburg 65, 73, 91
Austria 86, 96
Aycock, Alice, 125

Baskin, Leonard 123
Benguiat, Hadji Ephraim 8, 12
Berest, Deganit 117
Berghash, Mark 125
Berman, Wallace 126
Bezalel school 68
Bing and Grondahl 92
Bohemia 74, 95
Boller, Johann Adam 16, 67
Bonfils, La Maison 111
Borkovsky, Joshua 116

Chagall, Marc 104
Circumcision 86, 88
Copenhagen 92

Damascus 59
Danzig 54, 92

Edouart, August 101
England 90
Epstein, Jacob 106
Esther, Scroll of 72
Ethiopia 63

Fishman, Louise 123
France 42, 48
Frankfurt-am-Main 16, 41, 65, 67, 77, 82, 84
Friedman, Harry G. 13, 14

Galicia 50, 96
Ganbash, Moses 58
Gans, Jacob Koppel 38
Gerasimov, Andrej 83
Gerlovin, Valeriy 125
Gerlovina, Rimma 125
Germany 14, 52, 54, 59, 61, 63, 75, 84, 88
Gershuni, Moshe 115
Gieldzinski, Lesser 13
Goldstein, Georges 79
Gottlieb, Adolph 118
Gross, Michael 47, 116
Gurion, David Ben 20

Haan, Reymer de 67
Haggadah 60
Hannukah 60

Hannukah lamp 10, 16, 65, 66, 67, 68, 69, 70
Hart, Solomon Alexander 33
Hermans, Eduard 70
Hirszenberg, Samuel 103
Holland 14, 48, 67, 70, 72
Holocaust 112, 118
Hübener, Joachim 45
Hungary 47

Israel 100, 112
Israel, Ancient, 23, 24, 25, 27, 28
Istanbul 11, 30, 58
Italy 46, 52, 66, 90, 99

Jerusalem 68, 72, 79

Kadishman, Menashe 115
Kagan, Shirley 52
Kass, Deborah 126
Kayser, Stephen 17
Kaufmann, Isidor 81
Kiddush 83
Kirili, Alain 123
Kitaj, R. B. 119
Korshak, Max N. 13
Kupferman, Moshe 117

Lebrun, Rico 113
Lemberg (Lvov) 42, 46
Levy, Uriah Phillips 86, 99
Lipchitz, Jacques 16
Lissitzky, El 78
Los Angeles 70

Manievich, Abraham 104
Mannheim 89
Mantua 41
Marriage contracts 28, 86, 90
Meyer, Maurice 48
mezuzah 86, 96
Minkowski, Maurycy 102
Mintz, Benjamin 13
Mitterbacher, Joseph 92
Montreal 62
Murrow, Edward R. 20

Nadelman, Elie 106
Neustein, Joshua 114
New Jersey 70, 118
New Year, Jewish 60, 62
New York 52, 53, 57, 96, 99
Nuremberg 83, 94

omer 57, 79
Oppenheim, Moritz Daniel 102
Orloff, Chana 109
Ottolenghi, Leah 37
Ottoman Empire 28, 30, 41

Pap, Gyula 59
Parenti, Vincenzo 88
Passover 30, 60, 74, 75, 77
Persia, 42, 90
Petlin, Irving 124
Pilichowski, Leopold 65

Polacco, Rikah 52
Poland 76, 84
Polin, Burial Society of 95
Prague 92
prayer shawl 98
Pressman, Meichel 74
Preziosi, Amadeo 93
Prussia 56, 59
Purim, 60, 72, 73

Ring, Barukh Zvi 57
Rivers, Larry 120
Rockland, Mae Shafter 70
Rome 19, 88
Rosh Hashanah 60, 61
Rubin, Reuven 111
Russia 82, 83, 95, 98

Sabbath 80–85
Schiff, Jacob H. 12
Schiff Warburg, Frieda 12, 14
Schüler, Johann Valentin 65
Schulkin, Abraham 34
Schwartz, Maier 73
Seder 75, 76
Segal, George 17, 118
Segall, Laser 113
Shire, Peter 70
Shiviti 56, 58
Solomon, Solomon Joseph 65
Soutine, Chaim 107
Sukkot 60, 65
Sully, Thomas 101
Sulzberger, Mayer 9
Sultan, Larry 120
Syria 56, 59

tik 46, 48
Tissot, James Jacques Joseph 111
Torah 31–59, 60, 80, 89, 118; ark 11, 33, 34, 36, 37, 38; binder 31, 52, 53; crown 31, 42, 45; finials 31, 40, 41, 42, 46; mantle 31, 40, 41, 48, 50; pointer 31, 40, 52; shields 31, 41, 45, 46, 47
Tunisia 45

United States 62, 68, 99

Vienna 73, 75

Wagner, Zacharias 45
Warburg, Felix M. 12, 14
Weber, Max 108
Weil, Brian 120
Weiss, Johann Conrad 94
Weissburg, Sarah Eydel 72
Wild, Hans Jakob, II 91
Wilke, Hannah 120
Wolpe, Berthold 84
Wolpert, Ludwig 15, 19, 77
Worms, Burial Society of 94

Yom Kippur 60, 63

Zabari, Moshe 15, 99
Zobel, Jeremias 41